M000074531

# Care: You Have the Power!

## By Ivan Temes

20660 Stevens Creek Blvd., Suite 210
Cupertino, CA 95014

# Copyright © 2008 by Happy About®

First Printing: October 2008
Paperback ISBN: 1-60005-126-X (978-1-60005-126-5)
Place of Publication: Silicon Valley, California, USA
Paperback Library of Congress Number: 2008936650

eBook ISBN: 1-60005-127-8 (978-1-60005-127-2)

## Trademarks

## Warning and Disclaimer

# Praise for this Book

"These wonderful stories take the topic of *care* and teach us how we can make it front and center in our lives. I was inspired by the simplicity and power of the book and know that anyone who reads it will be equally impressed."
**Frederic Luskin, Ph.D.; author, *Forgive for Good*, Director, Stanford Forgiveness Projects**

"What an amazing concept Ivan Temes has introduced to us all—that through *care* we have the power! Too often we look at power as dominance over others rather than service to them. Ivan has caught the heart of a beautiful lesson that Mother Teresa taught us all—that service is love in action. Share this truly powerful book with business associates, friends and family. Let's all join with Ivan to create a caring revolution!"
**Brian Biro, America's Breakthrough Coach**

"Ivan has really hit on the importance of care—whether it be in our business or personal lives. He's a role model for the 21$^{st}$ century in business. Care is certainly a foundation of our rapid growth at *Joie de Vivre Hospitality*."
**Chip Conley, CEO, Joie de Vivre Hospitality**

"These stories are wonderful. Trust leads to motivation and participation. In *Care: You Have the Power* we should each be able to identify with and use the care factors that are the foundation of real trust."
**Bill Campbell, Chairman, Intuit Corporation**

"I loved your book. Many assume *care* is soft and takes too much time. You have made *care* clear, a tangible skill that can be relearned quickly and is a key to bottom line results."
**Lee Glickstein, President, Speaking Circles International**

"Wow, I am so impressed by your book and its fascinating insights and stories. It is so easy to read and does a wonderful job of reminding the reader of what is really important and acutely missing in the workplace of this country."
**Lisa Young, personal coach and healer**

## Author

- Ivan Temes
  http://ivantemes.com

## Publisher

- Mitchell Levy
  http://happyabout.info

## Editing & Layout

- Teclarity
  http://teclarity.com

## Cover Design

- Cate Calson
  http://CalsonGraphics.com/

iv

# Dedication

It's easy to dedicate this book to my three children, Josh, Kelly and Matt—those shining stars of *care* in my life.

As a college freshman last year, Kelly sent me a holiday card saying, "I look forward to shaking your hand when the book is finished." My teenage daughter demonstrated to me what *Care: You Have the Power* is about. I felt her care, was inspired and quickly ended my procrastination about finishing what I had started years ago.

At age 12, Josh commented to me, "Dad, don't talk to the reader." With his youthful wisdom he was letting me know that I should not list action steps at the end of each chapter. Let the reader interpret how the story fits in their life. I followed Josh's advice.

Matt has always encouraged me to get the stories into a written format.

Thanks to my children for their support in achieving my own dream.

# Acknowledgments

I feel particularly grateful to those many customer care personnel I was lucky to work with in organizations worldwide—and equally thankful to the thousands of seminar participants from homeless shelters and career transition groups. They were instrumental in my learning about the common denominators regarding *care* in all areas of our lives.

Craig Harrison, who had not seen my actual work, cared and believed in me enough after my many company layoffs and closures to refer me to Bill Dahl. I was then given the chance to begin a new path in life via developing and delivering a six-week *customer skills for hospitality* course at San Jose State University.

Mitchell Levy, publisher of Happy About, exemplifies *care* with his belief and commitment to the success of his authors.

Along the way, Reverend Jim Thomas, Skip Vaccarello, Libby Pannwitt, Allan Johnson, Roger Cruickshank and Lisa Young have been vigilant about encouraging me in this endeavor.

Lee Glickstein taught me the value of stories that touch the heart of an audience in any situation.

Many CEOs have been kind enough to contribute to the book and I'm particularly thankful to Hannah Kain, Bill Campbell and Chip Conley who have been very encouraging for the past five years.

# A Message from Happy About®

Thank you for your purchase of this Happy About book. It is available online at http://happyabout.info/care.php or at other online and physical bookstores.

- Please contact us for quantity discounts at sales@happyabout.info
- If you want to be informed by e-mail of upcoming Happy About® books, please e-mail bookupdate@happyabout.info

Happy About is interested in you if you are an author who would like to submit a non-fiction book proposal or a corporation that would like to have a book written for you. Please contact us by e-mail editorial@happyabout.info or phone (1-408-257-3000).

Other Happy About books available include:

- They Made It!:
  http://happyabout.info/theymadeit.php
- The Successful Introvert:
  http://happyabout.info/thesuccessfulintrovert.php
- 30day Bootcamp: Your Ultimate Life Makeover:
  http://happyabout.info/30daybootcamp/life-makeover.php
- 30day BootCamp to Eliminate Fears & Phobias:
  http://happyabout.info/30daybootcamp/fears-phobias.php
- Lessons About Life Momma Never Taught Us:
  http://happyabout.info/lessons-about-life.php
- Happy About Working to Stay Young:
  http://happyabout.info/working-to-stay-young.php
- 42 Rules™ of Employee Engagement:
  http://happyabout.info/42rules/employee-engagement.php
- Awakening Social Responsibility:
  http://happyabout.info/csr.php
- Foolosophy:
  http://happyabout.info/foolosophy.php
- Happy About Customer Service?:
  http://happyabout.info/customerservice.php
- 42 Rules™ for Working Moms:
  http://happyabout.info/42rules/workingmoms.php
- Blitz the Ladder:
  http://happyabout.info/blitz.php
- Happy About Being a Baby Boomer:
  http://happyabout.info/babyboomer/newfound-longevity.php

# Contents

## Chapter 4 | Children and Youth: Always an Opportunity . . . . . . . . . . . . . . . . . . . . . . . . 41

## Chapter 5 | From Sales to Shelters . . . . . . . . . . . . . . . . . 49

Contents

# Introduction to *Care*

*Care*—a simple word, or so it seems. This book will dispel that notion very quickly. *Care* may well be the most powerful word in the English language, perhaps surpassing *love*. This book is about *you* and the magnificent *care* tools already at your disposal. Perhaps, you have felt there is something missing in what has become to many people an impersonalized world of communication. Oprah Winfrey noted in an October 2001 editorial in her magazine that all the electronic devices we use make it difficult to really connect with each other.

Although this book and the contribution it could make had been a dream of mine for many years, I had pretty much decided to give up late last year. The *dream* seemed too much trouble. Then I received a holiday greeting card from my daughter Kelly, who had recently gone off to her first year of college. Kelly said, "I look forward to shaking your hand when the book is finished."

What an incredible feeling I had—that a teenager cared enough to support me and take some action to show that she cared. I had to move forward quickly. That's the essence of what this book is about—the simple caring actions that we can perform, and how they affect those around us positively—no matter what the circumstances.

In reality we truly are connected—all the time. The rediscovery of the skills imbedded in us at birth will very likely alter your life and relationships (business and personal) in ways you cannot yet even imagine.

My life's journey has taught me that this is possible. I had a strange experience when I was lying in the emergency room of Stanford Hospital on a Sunday morning in 2001, with a couple of IVs helping combat an infection. As I lay there, a bright light seemed to hover over me and a large, brown, rectangular medallion encompassed in flames appeared with the words *organizational healing* in the center. The picture is just as clear to me today as it was that Sunday morning. I imagined it meant I should embark on a path to train senior managers in how to build healthy organizations. However, my path since then has revealed a different message.

It's a direction which reinforces that a *star shines within each person*. When each of us feels cared for, our lives and our relationships with those around us are much more satisfying. We have much more control than we may realize. Where have some of these lessons come from? In my transition from the corporate world, I have led over 350 sessions related to *building confidence and marketing yourself* at homeless shelters, career centers and universities.

I was given the opportunity to work with homeless military veterans to assist them in gaining employment under difficult circumstances. I had what others called *an extraordinary success rate*. I knew it was much more about building caring relationships than simply job-hunting itself. I was right.

At the age of 60, I toiled as a janitor in the evenings, to help cover expenses for myself and my family. It's a story that I tell later in this book.

Previously, I had learned the ins and outs of the corporate world and all the fear and frustration that comes with the impersonal communication in many situations—having gone through several company closures myself.

I spent many years in international situations directing and managing groups for Levi's International and JBL International. I managed large teams at companies that included Apple Computer, Cisco, Oracle,

Navigation Technologies and Grid Systems. I experienced the dotcom purge at organizations that included MyTeam (Little League affiliation) and Privada (American Express affiliation). I also interacted with thousands of customers in retail environments.

My early mentors got across to me the importance of caring. In a service arena that is known for high-turnover rates, the retention rate of those in my organizations was well above 95%—even when the company was laying off hordes of people. This led to the publishing of my national article on *Maintaining Service Loyalty During a Downsizing.* Truly, the successes revolved around personnel feeling cared for.

There's a rose that blossoms within others when they truly feel our care. We *can* each make such a difference, and the stories and vignettes in *Care: You Have the Power* depict that message very clearly. *Care* is much more than a soft skill. As my friend Lee Glickstein, President of Speaking Circles International says, "I love your care book. Many assume care is soft and takes too much time. You have made *care* clear, a tangible skill that can be relearned quickly and is a key to bottom line results." I would add that it's also a key in communication with our children and friends.

What astounds me is the ease by which we can simplify and improve relationships with those around us in virtually any scenario.

Please prepare to be surprised by the simplicity of the message about *care.* I'm averse to books that tell us what others do to be successful and yet leave us wondering *how* to do it ourselves. The examples in *Care: You Have the Power* will allow you to easily understand what actions and steps you can take in your own situation.

What would life be like if those you met quickly said, "You're someone I can really trust. I want to be around you." Is that the case now? The evidence—particularly in the business world—indicates that is most assuredly not our experience.

Does it appear that everyone around us *cares?* Do they take action to show it? Each of us has the power to show *I care* and to positively affect conditions around us.

# These people know about *care* and results

William James, known as the father of American psychology, wrote that, "The deepest need of human beings is the desire to feel appreciated." I would add that it very much includes *care*. The individuals below represent a cross-section of people—CEO to Hall of Fame football player to homeless former journalist—who truly demonstrate how *care* fits in all areas of life.

- Steve Young, the Hall of Fame professional football quarterback from the San Francisco 49ers shares his eloquence on the topic—and an incredible result.

- A world-renowned chef from the San Francisco area gives his perspective on what creates exceptional loyalty and how it revolves around care and trust.

- Brian Biro, who travels nationally, inspiring audiences with his interactive sessions involving teamwork and growth, had a life-changing experience with his three-year-old daughter. Her astounding feedback symbolizes how care is such a critical factor in our relationships with children. The feedback from his daughter also enhanced Brian's ability to listen and impart messages to his audiences.

- A Silicon Valley CEO shares about *committing small murders* before discovering the care factor. She now spends five minutes a day that lead to her entire organization being more productive and loyal. Only five minutes does it.

- Mary, an award-winning national journalist, was temporarily living in a family shelter with her newborn baby when we met. Mary had the courage to speak out in caring ways that changed the lives of emigrants seeking new jobs. Mary took an extra step that is available to all of us.

- Bill Campbell, Chairman of the Board of Intuit Corporation and a former Apple Computer Executive Vice President of Sales and Marketing and football coach at Columbia University, demonstrates the one-minute version of *care* that can shift our relationships with everyone around us.

- Hal Rosenbluth, Chairman of Take Care Health Systems and who built Rosenbluth Travel from a $20 million enterprise to $5 billion, shares about the incredible value of a foundation of care and trust.

Webster's Dictionary even defines *spirit* in a way that shows care can be a key factor in areas of growth and development—*the animating life-force believed to be within living beings.* We can easily use the care factor to truly nurture and support those around us—and watch the positive results. More than the giving of care is that the receiver *feels* the care. That's when the growth sets in, personally or organizationally.

***Could it be this simple?*** **Emerson, Confucius and Buffett agree!**

*"Society is always taken by surprise by any new example of common sense."*
**Ralph Waldo Emerson**

*"Life is really simple and we insist on making it complex."*
**Confucius**

*"The business schools reward complex behavior more than simple behavior; simple behavior is more effective."*[1]
**Warren Buffett**

---

1. http://tinyurl.com/5wgtb9

Introduction

# 1 Caring and the First Impression

## Oprah Says it Best

In an October 2001 story in her magazine *Oprah*,[2] Oprah Winfrey uses her eloquence to reinforce the importance of personalizing our relationships in this computer-oriented society. Says Oprah:

> *"Having intimate connections with the people we love has never been more of a challenge. While cell phones, beepers, e-mail, the Internet and Palm Pilots make communication faster and more efficient, they also diminish the number of meaningful face-to-face interactions we have...*
>
> *...make it your goal not only to listen to others but to really hear them with all of your senses...let your children into your heart...connect in real time."*

The stories in *Care: You Have the Power* very much reinforce the point that Oprah makes so well.

---

2. Oprah Winfrey, *Heart to Heart*, O Magazine, October 2001

# The *Cs* Show the Way

**Warren Bennis**, distinguished professor of leadership at the University of Southern California, former president of the University of Cincinnati and author of *On Becoming a Leader*, lists his 4 *Cs* for success in organizations:[3]

- *Caring* (a foundation for *trust*)

- Consistency

- Competence

- Congruity

**Psychology for Business** (Wisconsin-based) notes a study that the 3 *Cs* were the key factors in organizations which had healthy climates. They included:

- Challenge

- Commitment

- Control

However, they had to add a fourth *C* based on the feedback they received:

- *Care*

Says Dr. John Weaver of *Psychology for Business,* "That seems to be the fate of *caring* in the workplace. It does not easily fit with our beliefs about business. We are uncomfortable with the thought that *caring* belongs in the workplace. We are even more uncomfortable with the idea that *caring* could be a key to being more successful and more profitable."

---

3. Warren Bennis, *On Becoming a Leader* (Perseus Books, 1989)

**Peter Taber**, Chairman of the chain of award-winning Hobee's restaurants in Northern California posts his 4 *Cs* for all to see:

- *Care*

- Customer

- Community

- Crew

Joanna Brandi, known as the *Customer Care Lady* for her work nationally says:[4]

- *Care*       **C**reate **A** **R**elationship with **E**veryone

Dr. Weaver also noted that when Suzanne Kobasa and Salvatore Maddi set out to do their research on the qualities of individuals who were emotionally healthy or *hardy* during times of stress, they theorized that the qualities of *commitment, challenge* and *control* would be the critical features. Indeed, they did observe those qualities and examined them in detail.

To their surprise, a fourth quality consistently emerged: *Caring*. In the interviews that were conducted with their original group of executives, they did not plan for nor did they systematically examine the dimension of *caring*. Its importance is even more striking because these emotionally healthy executives spontaneously and consistently named it as a quality that was essential in day-to-day work life. Other executives, who were far more susceptible to the stresses of the job and more likely to get sick, were much less likely to discuss the importance of caring in their workday.

---

4. http://customercarecoach.com

# John McCormack—*Action* is the Path

John McCormack, CEO of a highly-successful chain of Visible Changes hairstyle salons in Texas and author of *Self Made In America: Plain Talk for Plain People*[5] has built an organization with an extraordinary service commitment to its clientele.

John paid his dues and focuses on the *action* that demonstrates *care*.

Says John about *action*: "A misconception about *taking action* is that thinking, feeling or talking about something long enough will lead you to the *impulse* that will lead to action or forward motion.

In other words, if I think about something long enough, eventually, I'll get inspired enough to do it. Unfortunately, it doesn't work that way. In fact it's exactly the opposite.

Thinking and feeling do not produce action; action produces thinking and feeling. Once action has begun, it takes over and becomes unconscious—and this leads to an almost higher state of consciousness.

Psychologist Abraham Maslow called these results *peak experiences* and others have called the phenomenon simply *flow*.

Mark Twain put it another way, 'Thunder is good; thunder is impressive; it is lightning that gets the job done.'

We simply have to overcome the inertia in which we usually reside and make the initial effort to accomplish any task. And that's all. Our bodies and minds will take over from there. Remember, moving is actually easier than standing still."

While we may often care, it is our actions that translate the feeling of care to others. As John McCormack points out, "We need to take action first."

---

5. John McCormack, *Self Made In America: Plain Talk for Plain People* (Basic Books, 1992)

# Customers for Life!! All it Took was a Dead Bug

Our search for a family eatery while touring the Boston area led us to Au Bon Pain restaurant in Cambridge, Massachusetts. My spouse Naomi, son Matthew and young daughter Kelly had just arrived and were eagerly looking forward to seeing the historical sites in the area.

The order was taken, the sandwiches arrived and we began eating. Soon afterwards, Naomi walked back to the counter and quickly returned to her seat. I assumed she had a question which was answered by one of the hostesses.

About a minute later, a server came to our table, reached over and took Naomi's plate of food. I was aghast—wondering how someone could be that abrupt and have Naomi say nothing.

Five minutes later, the server returned with a plate of food and set it in front of Naomi, saying, "*That's* what we want you to have." I still had no idea what was taking place.

Then a lady with the nametag *Frankie* came over to our table, pulled up a chair and sat next to us. It turns out she was the restaurant manager. Frankie pulled out some money and said to Naomi, "Here's a refund for your family's *four* lunches. In case you want to come back and try us again, here are four lunch coupons for another visit. I want to apologize for the inconvenience. Thanks very much for your patience."

*Now*, I'm really wondering what is going on.

It turns out that Naomi's original sandwich had a teeny bug in it and she returned it to the counter, not wanting to have the children be concerned about the food.

As we were leaving I noticed a customer survey card with the name of Ron Shaich, CEO, on the card. I just *had* to know what created the type of responsiveness we received, so I managed to reach Ron on the phone and explained what had happened.

His reply, "I *care* a whole lot about my people. When we show them *caring* and support, they can—in turn—give the same to the customers."

Somehow Ron was able to drive that philosophy throughout his company. I know. My family and I were the beneficiaries.

Did a little bug in a sandwich, mixed with some *caring* turn me into a customer for life at Ron's restaurants? It sure did.

# Training *and Caring*—Missing the Target

How often have you sat in training classes and wondered what the value to yourself would be? Why were you there? How would you use the information?

Daniel Goleman, author of *Emotional Intelligence,* has a perspective on training that I believe hits the nail on the head in terms of what is really happening.

Goleman says that when the training is related to changes, the instructor may not be totally in tune with the uncertainty felt by the audience. It's possible that up to 80% of the room checks out when the session begins.

Change breeds uncertainly and fear. Before conducting trainings on this topic, it is necessary to gain a real understanding of the audience and what any potential change means to them—and then to *personalize* the information as much as possible. That will show that you *care* (even if management has not done this in its day-to-day interactions) and the audience will be more open to listening in the class. The group may well then participate more openly.

If we have done the research to show that we understand and care, our first impression with the audience will be much more likely to capture their attention—and hearts.

# Eat the Meal—it shows you care

Michelle Conlin, respected journalist and work/life editor for *Business Week*, says the best leader she has ever known was professor Dick Blood at Columbia University's School of Journalism.

Professor Blood had a unique way of teaching caring. His adage—*Eat the Meal*—is something Michelle says she has always held closely.

Professor Blood exhorted us to go to great lengths to learn everything we possibly could about the people we were covering. That meant sleeping on their sofas, shadowing them in their jobs and sitting down with them at dinner—no matter if we were vegetarians served a big plate of meat.

The professor taught us that by immersing ourselves in the tiny universe of the people we were entrusted to understand we could then reflect a slice of them to a larger world. It's an adage that inspires good reporting.

"*Eating the meal* has taught me how to stretch my vision, my empathy and my ability to service—rather than being served by my job."

Michelle is a reporter who learned her lesson well and who ensures her subjects feel *cared about. She listened and learned about them.*

# Customer, Care, Community and Crew—the Hobee's Way

Peter Taber's father, Paul, opened the first Hobee's restaurant in the San Francisco Bay Area in 1974.

**Customer, care, community and crew** have become the cornerstone of the business philosophy. Peter took over as company President and the business has grown to seven restaurants grossing over $12 million annually.

Peter said his dad believed *trust was the key component in building the business.* He also noted that *Your product has to be better than the next guy's—even if you are just serving eggs.*

Peter's leadership philosophy and his concern for the well-being of his employees has created an environment where *many* employees have been with the company for over 10 years—certainly well above the norm for the restaurant business.

The reason? Peter is adamant that you have to care deeply about every customer and team member and show that to them via your actions. One of the key reasons is that Peter includes all of management and employees in the company vision on a regular basis so they see themselves involved—in both good times and bad.

## Customers Helping Customers—What's Up at Hobee's?

As I waited for my serving of Hobee's famous coffeecake and their spiced tea, I could see that several customers were eating alone individually at several tables. One of them looked toward the waitress and signaled that he would like a glass of water. The waitress nodded her confirmation.

Quickly, another customer two tables away walked over to the requestor with his unused glass of water, saying he would not be drinking it.

Peter Taber also said it was important to his father that he built restaurants which operated with the highest level of integrity—and the organization has won many quality awards for their chain in Northern California.

Could Hobee's have built that unique environment where *everyone cares?* It certainly looked like it that day.

# 2 Disappearance of the Human Moment

### A Little Caring Brings it Back

## The Disappearance of the Human Moment

Ed Hallowell, noted psychiatrist, consultant and Harvard professor and also the father of three children stated in *The Harvard Business Review*[6] that, *The human moment has started to disappear in modern life. We may soon discover the power of its absence. Distrust and dissatisfaction are contagious. We see a deficiency of human contact via body language, tone and facial expressions.*

Dr. Hallowell is a renowned specialist in the field of ADD.[7] He very much humanizes himself when speaking to his audience. I personally experienced this when I heard him address a group of middle and high school parents in Menlo Park, California. Like Oprah, I believe he is alerting us

---

6. Dr. Ned *Ed* Hallowell, *The Human Moment at Work*, Harvard Business Review, Jan/Feb 1999
7. http://drhallowell.com/

to the needs to personalize our interactions. Dr. Hallowell's first impression with an audience is that *he cares.*

# Whew! Bringing Back the *Human Moment*

Joie de Vivre Hospitality or JDV Hospitality, under the strong guidance of chairman Chip Conley, has grown from one modest boutique hotel to over thirty properties in a rapid time frame. Jane Howard, Chief People Officer at JDV, says there are six key components to how the company creates such a vibrant and positive corporate culture and the most important of these is *hiring managers who care.* It's no coincidence that a foundation of *care* has led to significant company expansion and financial growth.

# Care is Not Just a Soft Skill; it is a Contributor to Our Success in any Business or Life Situation

I was leading a session recently for workers going through career transition in San Jose, California. Charles, one of the participants, just *knew* he needed to get away from the hotel and hospitality industry. He was very dissatisfied by the way he had been treated in all of his assignments in a wide variety of hospitality situations.

I listened to Charles harangue the industry and my intuition said that Charles really could use his experience effectively within a hotel. I doubted he had worked in an environment which demonstrated care and commitment to employees. I referred Charles to Jennifer, who recruits personnel for many of Chip Conley's properties. Here's the response I received from Charles three weeks later:

*Hi Ivan:*

*I'm at Hotel Los Gatos as a front desk host. I am finding it exciting, engaging and fun. The whole team is incredibly helpful and kind. The management team is way above what one could expect and desire. You were right—the perception I have had about hotels and hospitality was completely wrong.*

Is it any wonder that Chip's organization has grown so rapidly? Care is no secret there. Employees feel it—and so do the customers who often return. There are many *human moments*.

# The *Care* Formula for Success

Here's the *care formula* in a nutshell. Take this prescription for success and run with it in your life. Ensure that your caring results in people saying:

* I feel listened to.

* You told me the truth.

* You *care* about me.

* I *trust* you.

* I am loyal to you.

* I will be responsible in my dealings with you.

* I want to do my best for you while we are together.

# The Smile

In *Yes! Attitude,*[8] author Jeffrey Gitomer reinforces the importance of the smile and the very positive effect it has on a first impression that helps the other person or audience feel cared for.

Says Jeffrey: The smile brings the following benefits:

* It displays *positive* without saying a word

* It shows your warmth

* It shows your internal feelings, externally

* It shows you're happy

8. Jeffrey Gitomer, *Yes! Attitude* (Financial Times, 2007)

- It shows you're open

- It shows you're confident

- And it sets a tone for the first spoken words

# The Magic of *Personalized E-mail*

Given our challenges at Myteam of supporting thousands of Little League volunteers in organizations and putting their leagues into an online format for the Internet, it was clear we would need people with patience and great attitudes to support our customers. Caring would need to be a key word in practice.

When I took over as Director of Customer Care I had little experience with the Internet. I did know how frustrated I was by the many *black holes of non-response* when I communicated with companies via e-mail. I was determined that we could do better. We could somehow respond on a more timely basis and show people that we cared about each of their individual inquiries.

Step One was finding some great—albeit inexperienced—front-line personnel with a strong dose of common sense. Step Two was to figure out how we could use our undermanned organization to handle the plethora of inquiries and still maintain a personalized approach.

In order to survive we had to utilize some standard responses—which often seem impersonal to the receiver. My instructions to the representatives were to *put something of themselves* into the response, and I left it at that.

As we moved forward, Manda, our most junior customer care representative, in her first *real job* after graduating from the University of California, Davis, began to receive a high number of compliments from Little League volunteers. Many of them were sent directly to me.

Although I fostered a *trusting* rather than *big brother is watching over you* environment, I had to see first-hand what Manda was doing.

The answer came quickly that afternoon with an e-mail inquiry from one of our Midwestern Little League volunteers. *Thank you for the quick response to my question. And thank you very much for asking how I was feeling. I've never communicated by e-mail with anyone who seemed to care so much.*

Manda had remembered that in the last communication, her customer was preparing for a minor operation. When the next communication arrived, Manda simply added her personal concerns in the response.

It should be so obvious what works. *Caring* at this level from the front-line could be contagious—and add to customer acquisition and loyalty in any environment.

## We do Have the Power in *Caring*

We can always ensure those around us feel cared for—if we choose to look past whatever other feelings we may have at the time.

**Ivan Temes, 2008**

## Social Isolation Growing—Throw in some *Care*

An article in 2006 by Shankar Vedantam in the Washington Post[9] noted that:

*Americans are far more socially isolated today than they were two decades ago, and a sharply growing number of people say they have no one in whom they can confide, according to a recent evaluation on social ties in the United States.*

---

9. Shankar Vedantam, *Social Isolation Growing In U.S.*, Washington Post, 6/23/06

*A quarter of Americans say they have no one with whom they can discuss personal troubles, more than double the number from a similar study in 1985.*

*In bad times far more people seem to suffer alone.*

Lynn Smith-Lovin, a Duke University sociologist, helped conduct the study and adds, "There really is less of a safety net of close friends and confidants. If a spouse falls sick, people often have no one to turn to for help."

However, the evidence is growing that a little listening and a little caring can go a long way in the lives of those around us. Dean Ornish, the well-known physician who has had dramatic results in working with patients on a diet and reversing heart disease, adds some confirming thoughts in his book *Love and Survival: The Scientific Basis for the Healing Power of Intimacy.*[10]

In an article by Rebecca Ostriker, Ornish noted that, *Real intimacy can lead to emotional and spiritual transformation. Not just romantic intimacy. Intimacy is anything that takes you out of the experience of being separate. It could be with friends, family, lovers, pets, plants or God.*

"Factors to intimacy include **caring communication**, group support, commitment, touch and compassionate service," says Ornish.

# Caring. . .and the Lightbulb Inside Each of Us

On some occasions when I go into one of my bank branches, the attitude of the teller is somewhat less than upbeat.

However, I was awakened from my own lethargy one morning at Great Western (now Washington Mutual) Bank in Palo Alto when I received a very enthusiastic, "How may I help you? I'd love to provide whatever assistance you need."

10. Dean Ornish, *Love and Survival: The Scientific Basis for the Healing Power of Intimacy (Harper-Collins, 1998)*

I peered over the counter at the young man and saw via his nametag that I was speaking with *Robert.*

The entire interaction with Robert continued as enthusiastically as it had begun. I left smiling and feeling good from being *cared for* by a stranger in the bank.

I then strolled over to the branch manager's desk and learned she was the Vice President, Barbara Gross. I just had to know what Barbara was doing in her operation—in a bank—to generate such motivation from her personnel.

Barbara's answer was unique, "My biggest challenge is having people who may never have personally received exceptional service give great service to customers and really show they *care.*"

That's when my light bulb went on. Barbara is so right. It's difficult to teach a concept. Barbara had set up creative, interactive training programs which allowed each of her employees to personally experience the caring feeling that is translated to customers.

She is also very supportive of her people, encouraging them to learn from any mistakes. Leadership is *caring in action.*

Barbara demonstrated that philosophy so well that the upscale Garden Court Hotel in Palo Alto chose her to be their first general manager.

# A CEO Finds his Way to *Caring*—at a Prison

While singing hymns when visiting a prison, Cepheid CEO Tom Gutshall had an experience that revolutionized the way he treats and manages people.

In 1970, a friend from church asked Gutshall to help him lead hymns at the St. Louis County Prison. Gutshall admits he went in *a little judgmental about what these people were about.* However, sometimes meeting face-to-face with the unknown is enlightening.

Behind seven locked doors in a concrete cell with more than 40 inmates, Gutshall says, "God got my attention. It was as if I could actually hear the words."

*He* said, "You're all the same in terms of how I view you," Gutshall recalls. The CEO then resolved to convey that revelation in the way he manages people and lives his life. "I knew I needed to demonstrate to people that I truly cared about their well-being."

"That changed my whole perspective on business," says Gutshall. "I went back to work a different person. I'll now take one person's strength and back up another's weakness, treat people as teams, let them be part of the decision-making process, empower them to do what they do best—and then get out of the way."

It certainly appears to be working. Gutshall has leapt from one top management position to another at some of the country's largest chemical and pharmaceutical corporations.

Since 1986, Gutshall, who also won a college football scholarship, has been Chairman of the Board of City Team Ministries, a San Jose-based non-profit which also serves the needy around the world. City Team President Pat Robertson says that Gutshall *can be decisive and firm in his leadership—and also caring, gentle and compassionate.*

When Syntex consolidated its San Jose subsidiary, Syva Company, and laid off about 200 people, guess who was the hatchet man? Gutshall, of course.

According to Robertson, it was a nasty time. However, personnel commented that Tom exercised his role with incredible grace. People said they knew he *cared about them* on a personal basis.

From a visit to a prison to the real world. Tom Gutshall took in the *caring lesson* and passed it on.

# Care Enough to Remember My Name

One of the handouts I received from Amacom,[11] a division of the American Management Association, depicted one of life's important lessons to me. The story told—from an anonymous source—goes like this:

*During my second month of college, our professor gave us a pop quiz. I was a conscientious student and had breezed through the questions, until I read the last one: "What is the first name of the woman who cleans the school?" Surely this was some kind of joke. I had seen the cleaning woman several times. She was tall, dark-haired and in her 50s—but how would I know her name? I handed in the paper, leaving the last question blank. Just before class ended, one student asked if the last question would count toward our quiz grade. "Absolutely," said the professor. "In your careers you will meet many people. All are significant. They deserve your attention and **care**, even if all you do is smile and say 'hello.' I've never forgotten that lesson. I also learned her name was Dorothy."*

That story really hit home for me. During one of my transitional periods, I took on a three-night-a-week custodial position at a dentist's office. In the 1.5 years there I must have emptied the many garbage cans in the offices over 3,000 times and swept and mopped the nine individual offices over 250 times—sometimes on my hands and knees to get the grit off the floor. I was over 60 years of age at the time.

How often was I given a *thank you* from a single person in the large staff? Not once. Not even one time.

A great opportunity for each of us is to acknowledge the cleaning person wherever we may be. They will see that we care and will feel better for the small bit of appreciation.

---

11. http://amanet.org/books/

# The *Love Professor* and Cared for Rats

The late Leo Buscaglia, a professor at the University of Southern California and author of many holistic health books, was known for his inspiration, perspiration and propensity to lovingly hug people who came up to him after speeches.

He cited what he called the *rat test*. Two groups of rats were given fats. Only one was given attention. The one given attention showed results with the equivalent of lower cholesterol. Buscaglia concludes with, *Perhaps affection and care even lower cholesterol.*

In a survey about primary relationships quoted in his book *Loving Relationships*[12] respondents listed the following as the ten most important factors in primary relationships:

- Communication

- Affection

- Forgiveness

- Honesty

- Vulnerability

- Dependability

- Sense of Humor

- Romance

- Patience

- Freedom

I would presume *communication* is number one because the *care factor* is such an important factor—listening so that others feel cared for.

---

12. Leo Buscaglia, *Loving Relationships* (Ballantine, 1985)

# This Cab Driver Took the Long Route

This cab driver demonstrated the power of caring within each of us to make a real impact in the life of another. The story of the Cab Driver[13] goes like this:

*Twenty years ago, I drove a cab for a living. When I arrived at 2:30 a.m., the building was dark except for a single light in a ground floor window. Under these circumstances, many drivers would just honk once or twice, wait a minute, and then drive away. However, I had seen too many impoverished people who depended on taxis as their only means of transportation. Unless a situation smelled of danger, I always went to the door. This passenger might be someone who needs my assistance, I reasoned to myself.*

*I walked to the door and knocked. "Just a minute," answered a frail, elderly voice. I could hear something being dragged across the floor. After a long pause, the door opened. A small woman in her 80s stood before me. She was wearing a print dress and a pillbox hat with a veil pinned on it, like somebody out of a 1940s movie. By her side was a small nylon suitcase. The apartment looked as if no one had lived in it for years. All the furniture was covered with sheets. There were no clocks on the walls, no knickknacks or utensils on the counters. In the corner was a cardboard box filled with photos and glassware.*

*"Would you carry my bag to the car?" she asked. I took the suitcase to the cab, then returned to assist the woman.*

*She took my arm and we walked slowly toward the curb. She kept thanking me for my kindness. "It's nothing," I told her. "I just try to treat my passengers the way I would want my mother treated."*

*When we got to the cab, she gave me an address, then asked, "Could you drive through downtown?"*

*I said, "It will take longer."*

*"I don't mind," she said. "I'm in no hurry. I'm on my way to a hospice."*

---

13. Kent Nerburn, *Make Me An Instrument of Your Peace*, Harper, 1984

*I looked in the rearview mirror. Her eyes were glistening. "I don't have any family left," she continued. "The doctor says I don't have very long."*

*I quietly reached over and turned off the meter. "What route would you like me to take?" I asked.*

*For the next two hours we drove through the city. She showed me the building where she once worked as an elevator operator. We drove through the neighborhood where she and her husband had lived when they were newlyweds. She had me pull up in front of a furniture warehouse that had once been a ballroom where she had gone dancing as a girl. Sometimes she'd ask me to slow down in front of a particular building or corner and would sit staring into the darkness, saying nothing.*

*As the first hint of the sun arrived, she suddenly said, "I'm tired. Let's go now."*

*We drove in silence to the address she had given me. It was a low building, like a small convalescent home. Two orderlies came out to the cab as we pulled up. They were solicitous and intent, watching her every move. They must have been expecting her.*

*I opened the trunk and took the small suitcase to the door. The woman was already seated in a wheelchair. "How much do I owe you?" she asked, reaching into her purse.*

*"Nothing," I said.*

*"You have to make a living," she answered.*

*"There are other passengers," I responded. Almost without thinking, I bent and gave her a hug. She held on to me tightly.*

*"You gave an old woman a little moment of joy," she said. "Thank you."*

*I squeezed her hand and walked into the dim morning light. Behind me a door shut. It was the sound of a closing of a life. I drove aimlessly, lost in thought, the rest of the day. What if that woman had gotten an angry driver, or one who was impatient? What if I had refused to take the run, or honked once and driven away?*

*I don't think I have ever done anything more important in my life. We're conditioned to think that our lives revolve around great moments. However, great moments often catch us unaware—beautifully wrapped in what others may consider a small one.*

**People will remember that we cared and how we made them feel.**

Chapter 2: Disappearance of the Human Moment

# 3 From *Committing Small Murders* to Caring CEO

## A CEO Goes from *Committing Small Murders* to *Caring*

Hannah Kain is a wise and successful Chief Executive Officer at ALOM Technologies in Northern California.

She says that a speaker at a TEC (organization of company presidents) event taught her about the *small murders* which we inadvertently commit.

A *small murder* is committed when the CEO hurriedly passes by the receptionist while deep in thought and does not greet or make eye contact.

OR when a *thank you* or small recognition is not made...

OR when someone is criticized in public...

Says Hannah, "I stopped committing small murders after hearing the term. It has made a real difference.

When I stepped into the company cafeteria, I used to head directly for whatever caused me to go there. Now I:

- Pause for five seconds

- Make eye contact with everyone

- Smile

- Then proceed

It probably takes me less than five minutes a day. However, I feel that I connect better with everyone in the company. People also tend to relax more around me, which is pleasant for me. This actually causes our employees to perform better."

*Wow!* Five minutes a day of *caring* from a CEO and everyone performs better. Our quality programs, which are often buried in the numbers, would love to make a statement like that.

# *Caring*—It Goes With the Egg Rolls

Chef Chu's is a well-known Chinese restaurant in Los Altos, California—nestled about halfway between San Francisco and San Jose. The tables are covered elegantly, serpents hang from the ceiling and a massive collage of the Great Wall of China adorns the entire back wall.

When you peer into the open view kitchen, you often see about 20 chefs bustling about excitedly creating their own specialty dishes. Then a waiter—equally enthusiastic—rushes the hot food out to a table of eagerly awaiting patrons.

All the workers seem to be aligned like ants in a colony, each ensuring their personal task is of the highest quality so the team can be successful. The customers reap the rewards of the tantalizing food.

When I asked Larry Chu Jr., a UCLA graduate and son of the owner/chef who founded the business, what creates an environment where the workers always appear to be so highly motivated, he did not hesitate with the answer.

Said Larry Jr., "My father does all of the work that each of the other employees does. He enjoys being with his staff and they know he *cares* about them individually."

Could "Leadership is caring *in action*" be that simple?

A resounding, "Yes, it could be—and it is."

Just taste those egg rolls.

# Listen—a Simple Formula

Roger Meade in his role as CEO at Scitor Corporation had a reputation for ensuring his personnel felt cared for. Said Roger:[14]

- To increase productivity, first you need to understand the human heart.

- Knowing how to stir the passion fuels productivity.

- *Start* with *Listening*—every stupid thing happens when we don't talk to our people about their projects. Roger also ensured he or his management took appropriate action when necessary.

# One-on-One—You do Have Control

Company senior management are the ones who contribute *most* to employee motivation and loyalty? Right? Or maybe wrong?

The one-on-one relationship between an employee and their direct supervisor has a *greater impact on motivation and loyalty* than any other dynamic taking place in an organization.

Think of the times you were loyal to someone. Did it seem like they listened and cared—and sometimes could take action?

That's what I did. The result—a 95 per cent employee retention record over 15 years—even when companies were known to be closing in the near future.

---

14. Roger Meade, *Running on People Power*, Industry Week, Oct. 18, 1993

Don't fall into that blame or *it's hopeless* game with employees who work for you.

Stand tall. Be positive. Listen. Demonstrate that you care. Everyone will feel at least a little better.

# Park at the Back Door

Rick LeBlanc has had chief executive roles in several industries—including semiconductor and telecommunications. His real-world philosophy, accompanied by Action—encourages openness and creativity from *all* employees.

Rick recognizes the walls that often permeate organizations and become a de-motivating factor to employees who want to maximize their contribution to the company. He also knows from experience that *actions* speak much louder than words.

He takes matters into his own hands when it comes to *demonstrating* to employees that he is serious about wanting to hear from them.

Rick's adage: **Park at the back door**

Rick does not enter the company via the front door and head to his office. He intentionally parks at the back door, closest to a manufacturing or production facility.

He then strolls past the cubicles and work areas, often stopping to ask employees how things are going and listening to their ideas. He does not just listen. Rick takes notes, and often these ideas are a gateway toward enhancing productivity or quality.

What else happens? Employees take it upon themselves to proactively head to Rick's office—with or without an appointment. If he's available, he *always* takes the time to hear the ideas they want to share. Morale, retention and the sharing of creative ideas are maximized in Rick's organization. Listening and *caring in action* from the top goes a lot further than most formalized productivity improvements ever go. The foundation of trust has been established.

Simple? I would say so.

# Rethinking How We Show Care

Albert Einstein:[15]

**We cannot solve our problems with the same thinking we used when we created them.**

# General Colin Powell's Primer on *Leadership and Caring*

General Colin Powell, in Lesson 2 of his presentation *A Leadership Primer*[16] speaks out regarding an often-failed leadership opportunity:

"The day soldiers stop bringing you their problems is the day you have stopped leading them. They have either lost confidence that you can help them or concluded that you do not care. Either case is a failure of leadership."

"If this were a litmus test, the majority of CEOs would fail. One, they build so many barriers to upward communication that the very idea of someone lower in the hierarchy looking up to the leader for help is ludicrous. Two, the corporate culture they foster often defines asking for help as weakness or failure—so people cover up their gaps and the organization suffers accordingly.

Real leaders make themselves accessible and available. They show concern for the efforts and challenges faced by underlings, even as they demand high standards. Accordingly, they are more likely to create an environment where problem analysis replaces blame."

Powell adds, "Good leadership encourages everyone's evolution."

---

15. http://brainyquote.com/quotes/quotes/a/alberteins121993.html
16. http://blaisdell.com

# Why Should I Care? My Boss Doesn't

Who would make the above statement? One of my true mentors and idols.

While she will remain anonymous, she was a successful Vice President at two of the leading financial software companies in the United States—winning awards for outstanding service. She later moved on to a Chief Operating Officer role at another major corporation in Silicon Valley—jaded by the bureaucracy and corporate politics of so many organizations.

What happened to another one of my wonderful mentors—a senior manager reporting directly to the president of a major communications software company—a lady who had helped drive her previous corporation to a national quality award?

As I walked into her office for a meeting, she appeared downcast.

"What happened," I asked?

"I've just been laid off by the president—by *e-mail*," she exclaimed.

No wonder both of these highly-accomplished people asked me why I still care.

# Faster than an Instant

At my local hair salon, Bocca's, I was talking to the upbeat owner, June Wilson, about what keeps her people so happy and focused on their customers.

June simply utilized the philosophy of listening and caring for her people so they could do likewise for their many loyal customers.

However, June's daughter had a much more negative experience at her most recent company.

Says June, "My daughter had a reputation for being upbeat and happy."

One morning the company president walked by and saw her cheerful smile.

For whatever reason, he blurted out, "It's not my job to make you happy. You can stop smiling now."

What did June's daughter do? What could she do? She was devastated and quit. I would imagine customers of a company like this did likewise.

# Individual Caring Beats any System

When I was going through a job transition—all part of the many down-sizing scenarios after the dotcom bust in Silicon Valley—I had the occasion to call an organization chartered with providing funding for one of my transition programs.

As expected, I spent a significant amount of time on hold because of the sheer volume of participants involved.

Then a cheerful voice came on the phone, stating that she was Sarah and how might she help me. Sarah did a wonderful job of explaining some of my options and answering questions.

I asked her if I might write a letter to her superior for the great support she had given me.

Her answer, "Oh, no, that's OK. I love doing it. Besides, my management here does not really care."

Whether management cared or not, Sarah *cared* big time and I felt relieved and inspired after I spoke with her. The *Sarah's* of service are truly the backbone of an organization—often a key reason why a company does repeat business.

However, this case demonstrated an opportunity often available to us in difficult circumstances.

# Care and Suffering—Become a Winner

Pete Thigpen, a former President of Levi Strauss Europe, ethics processor at the Haas School of Business at the University of California Berkeley and a leader at the Aspen Institute in Colorado puts *caring* in a perspective that can be very meaningful in our lives.

Says Pete:

> *Really believe in your heart of hearts that your fundamental purpose, the reason for being, is to enlarge the lives of others. Your life will be enlarged also. And all of the things we have been taught to concentrate on will take care of themselves.*

I have often said that when we are feeling down or alone, one of the best antidotes is to simply do something for someone else.

**Demonstrate that we care personally while seeing past whatever else might be going on around us. We will feel better and the people with whom we are communicating will feel better. In that way each of us can often make a small difference to those with whom we may be communicating.**

# Nurses and Doctors—Equalizing the Training

One Silicon Valley hospital had initiated a mandatory *relationship training* class for both nurses and doctors.

The nurses were expected to do the three hours of training on their own time—and could earn some extra credits for doing so.

The doctors? They were allowed to take the class during their half-hour lunch break.

Did the nurses feel *cared for* in this situation? Of course not.

All management would have needed to do was to talk with the nurses before implementing the program and they would have discovered several potential alternatives.

Remember the equation:

- I feel listened to

- I know you care

- I trust you

- I am loyal

# Drive Out Fear with Some Caring—Stop the Epidemic

In their book *Driving Fear Out of the Workplace*[17] authors Kathleen Ryan and Daniel Oestreich discussed results of interviewing employees in 350 companies.

While *all* participants indicated they wanted to contribute to the success of the company, seven out of ten employees also said they withheld creative ideas because they felt that *no one cared* or that there might be retribution of some type.

From my experience, therein lies the key of turning around what is an epidemic in business and other arenas. People do not feel appreciated or cared for. We have an epidemic of people leaving companies. This issue is very fixable and will save millions of dollars in such areas as employee turnover.

**We most assuredly don't need many of those corporate consultants or training programs. When we show we simply *care* we establish environments and relationships which bring forth increased participation.**

How do we do that? Simply follow the care formula in Chapter 2 in this book. It will take some practice. When people see you are serious, they will aid you in developing an optimal communication process.

---

17. Kathleen D. Ryan and Daniel K. Oestreich, *Driving Fear Out of the Workplace* (Jossey-Bass, 1991)

# A CEO's Risky Way to Show Sales She Cared

Many of us have been in organizations where the reality of what was happening was somewhat different than what management **said** was the reality of the situation.

Such was the case at Advanced Cardiovascular Systems (ACS) when Ginger Graham took over as CEO and had an early assignment to address a national sales force—and their skepticism about another change at the senior level.

Ginger did not waver. As noted in a national magazine,[18] she stood up and told the absolute truth about what was happening—that research and development was practically at war with product development, yields were down and customers were disgruntled.

Truth telling is hard to argue with and sometimes difficult to do in organizations. Ginger's willingness to start with the truth quickly won her the trust of the sales organization. They could *strongly feel how much she cared about the success of the company.*

ACS instituted some radical practices to create its culture of honesty. Every senior manager was assigned a coach from the rank-and-file who regularly solicited feedback—high and low—about the executive's performance.

To get to the truth, ACS executives learned they had to offer it up themselves—the whole truth about the company's financial status, its problems and its triumphs.

Passive employees became active partners in the fortunes of the company.

Regular ACS senior management meetings were held where all participants provided feedback to one another and pushed for improved performance—to keep them honest and tough enough to go on telling the truth. In the process of openly owning problems and jointly fixing them

---

18. http://harvardbusinessonline.hbsp.harvard.edu

with employees, the entire company grew more powerful, nimble and tough-minded. It was able to respond quickly to both internal and external change.

Where did it begin? With a CEO who *cared enough to tell the truth.*

# Rebuilding Trust in an Instant of Caring

I woke up that September morning with what seemed to be a severe cold and was sure this was not a day to get out of bed. One issue—I had been given an opportunity to address the national field sales meeting of 200 attendees for the Grid Systems national conference near San Francisco.

Grid, which was known for its excellent laptop computers, was going through a difficult period—having just been purchased by Tandy Corporation from Texas. I was to speak to a skeptical sales force about what a great job service could do in partnership with them.

Given the history, there was not much I could say that would alter their negative perceptions about the service and support they and their nationwide customers received from the West Coast office. However, I don't give up easily. After all I had prepared a talk with lots of colorful slides.

Although I was new as the customer service manager, I had already called the regional sales personnel to see how we might improve our overall response; however, some of them were still reluctant to give the direct service number to their customers.

I listened to other talks at the conference—covering products and promising better times ahead. Then it was my turn, stuffed head notwithstanding.

I took my presentation, peered out at the large audience and—on the spur of the moment—set my prepared notes on the floor. I chose instead to let my heart speak the truth—not quite sure of what to say. Quickly I jumped into a *Bob Newhart-type dialogue* using it to illustrate the reality of the perceptions amongst the sales group. I then proceeded to commit to everything the sales force wanted for their customers from a superior service organization—even adding a few items they might not have thought possible.

Then I peered at Betsy, one of the regional managers, in the front row and looked around at an audience that included six future company presidents. Betsy rose and cheered, acting as if she had finally heard a true commitment about what was needed. The entire audience then rose as one, clapping and cheering.

I was dumbfounded and did my best to smile through the emotions I was feeling. After all what had I done? I committed to what I knew could be achieved—via trust, teamwork, partnerships and a strong dose of *caring*.

Did it work? Three months later came an e-mail from one of the national sales regions stating that, *We truly were reluctant to give out the customer service number. Now we believe we have a team behind us that other companies would die to have.*

I can see that CEO Ginger Graham was right when *she* began with the truth to a skeptical sales force at her company, Advanced Cardiovascular Systems. They saw she too cared and the results later reflected that to be the case.

# 4 Children and Youth: Always an Opportunity

## The Caring Factor with Children and Youth

We have seen the importance of *listening* as part of the *care factor.* When I mentioned listening to my 12-year-old son Josh he said, "Dad, I can't listen. I always want to say the next thing." What wisdom from Josh. He was pretty much speaking for the world as it exists around us. He also reinforced that *honesty* is a key component in our ability to trust others.

It did not matter whether Josh was right or wrong. It did matter that Josh was honest and I could trust his words. In other environments that factor reinforces *care.* Once again, simplicity reigns.

## Listening? Caring? Our Children Know the Difference

Brian Biro is a masterful motivational speaker who travels nationally. He is very skilled at using exercises that ensure his audience is charged up, participating and focused on their own goals in life.

He imparts *caring* in his own way and quickly builds trust with his audiences.

However, Brian's schedule was keeping him from having a sufficient amount of time at home with his three-year-old daughter Jenna. A frustrated Brian told Jenna, "Next time I'm home I'll spend lots of time with you."

After his next trip Brian embarked on keeping his word with Jenna. They sat in her room amongst her favorite dolls and toys. With a twinkle in his eye, Brian looked over at Jenna and said, "I'm here with you. Isn't that great?"

Jenna saw the situation differently, "No, you're not here with me, Daddy. You're on the telephone."

A painful emotional experience for Brian. "I felt like I had been punched in the jaw." A real life lesson that all of us should be able to learn from. Guess who turns his cell phone off when he is on the floor playing with his daughter now? Who wins?

It is not so much that we care; rather it is the giving of it through our actions and how the other person *feels our caring* that is important.

Open our ears. Close our mouths. Watch how our relationships work at that point.

With children, go to their level. Do you realize the little ones see a lot of adult knees when they are walking around? Kneel down. Speak to children at their level, eye-to-eye, smile-to-smile.

I noticed that when I was doing retail work at Gap Kids I often kneeled down to the younger children. No big deal to me. However, it often led to parents returning and mentioning to me—and the manager—how nice it was that someone cared enough to personalize the interaction with their child. Yes, *caring* can equate to revenue.

# Harsh Words and a Child[19]*

I ran into a stranger as he passed by,
"Oh excuse me" was my reply.
He said, "Please excuse me too; I wasn't watching for you."
We were polite, this stranger and I
We went on our way and we said good-bye.
But at home a different story is told,
How we treat our loved ones, young and old.
Later that day, cooking the evening meal,
My son stood beside me very still.
When I turned, I nearly knocked him down,
"Move out of the way," I said with a frown.
He walked away, his little heart broken—there was no *care*
I didn't realize how harshly I'd spoken.
While I lay awake in bed,
God's still small voice came to me and said,
"While dealing with a stranger, common courtesy you use,
But the children you love, you seem to abuse.
Go look on the kitchen floor,
You'll find some flowers there by the door.
Those are the flowers he brought for you.
He picked them himself, pink, yellow and blue.
He stood very quietly not to spoil the surprise,
And you never saw the tears that filled his little eyes."
By this time, I felt very small,
And now my tear began to fall.
I quietly went and knelt by his bed;
"Wake up, little one, wake up," I said.
"Are these the flowers you picked for me?"
He smiled, "I found 'em out by the tree.
I picked 'em because they're pretty like you.
I knew you'd like'em, especially the blue."
I said, "Son, I'm very sorry for the way I acted today.
I shouldn't have yelled at you that way."
He said, "Oh, mom, that's okay, I love you anyway."
I said, "Son, I love you too,
And I do like the flowers, especially the blue."

---

19. http://Angelfire.com/journal2/cp_lai/harsh.htm
  * Anonymous poem

# Creative College Cramming—with a *Caring* Administrator

Linda Michels in her role as a college administrator has often been challenged with finding time to personalize the interactions with her students amidst their very busy schedules—particularly as the dates for final exams approached.

In her role at the Graduate Theological Union, Linda was in a position to change the focus of the graduate school from meeting the needs of the office to meeting the needs of the students. Language exams are required for graduate degrees—one language for an MA and two for a Ph.D.

Linda says that, "Due to the esoteric and ancient languages required for study of religion, the exams were not standardized and were dreaded by the students. Shortly before the date of the exams, one of my work-study students (a Ph.D. candidate) said something to the effect of, 'Maybe they wouldn't be so bad if we had milk and cookies.' So I brought graham crackers and apple juice to the exam room.

I also told the students they could leave when they were finished, that they didn't have to wait for others to finish. I wasn't interested in their being able to sit still; I wanted to know if they could translate their language. The students were so happy; you would have thought I had passed their exams for them.

All it took was a little indication of caring on my part."

Linda's actions certainly were caring and laced with common sense.

# Did this Professor *Care*?

The other side of the equation regarding Linda and her college class was uttered by a large business school graduate student.

He commented that, "The science professor always wants us to do more and more. I simply need to feel some appreciation for the work I have already done. Although it sounds stupid, I would feel differently inside. I would like to know that someone really *cares*."

Perhaps the student would benefit from a philosophy that I have seen work magnificently in many situations.

**Start with a positive or reaffirming statement and follow with any other feedback.**

# Keeping Your Word—Your child is on the corner waiting.

**Just do what you say you are going to do!**

One of the most important credos in business and life—particularly if you want to ensure that people know you care—is to follow through on your promises and commitments.

Rick LeBlanc, a CEO of several companies, drives home the importance of this message.

Your spouse calls and says, "I can't pick up Susie from school. Can you get her?"

Your answer, "Sure, I will get her."

Your spouse then says, "Okay, she will be ready at 4 p.m. and waiting at the curb."

You have made a promise, a commitment to pick up your daughter at 4 p.m. It is *not* acceptable to be late or not to pick her up. In this case, if you cannot fulfill your promise, you need to call your spouse or make other arrangements for Susie.

*For sure*, someone needs to be there to pick up Susie. In other words, the project has to be completed as promised. Susie is depending on you.

The same applies in business. When you agree to take an assignment, make sure you can do it and then do what you say you're going to do. If it turns out that you can't do it for some reason (or cannot meet the deadline) get back to the person before the deadline so other arrangements can be made.

It is not acceptable to let the deadline pass or not do the assignment. Someone else is depending on you.

Maintain trust by keeping your word. That's a clear demonstration that you *care*.

# From a 4-year-old—Get Up and Try Again

As I watched my son Joshua whiz around the ice-skating rink, I was drawn to the attempts of a young girl to stay on her feet while on the ice.

That's when Caroline—who is four years old—came over to her mother, "When you fall down, it's because you're trying hard. Then you get up and try again."

Caroline's wise, and obviously caring, mom just smiled and showed her support.

Sometimes that's all we need. A person who listens and shows they care. We feel a little stronger when we go for the objective again and—this time—stay on our feet.

# Show Care to the Children and See the Customers Return

It's never inconvenient for me to drive a little out of the way to have breakfast at the Village Pantry in Los Altos, California.

How can it be when the effervescent owner Julie always bursts out with a welcoming, "Hi" no matter who comes through the door? Somehow she always remembers the returning customers and calls out to them by name. Even if one of my children has not been there for a while she welcomes them by name also.

When I was speaking to a customer with three of her children in a booth, she affirmed that Julie *knows all of our names*. This group was getting ready to take out their boxes of left over food. On the top of each box was a hand drawn *smiley face*—put there by Julie, of course.

Care. Personalization. Returning customers. Revenue. Julie and her staff show us how to do it. She also serves what may be the best breakfast in the area.

It did not take long for a visiting newspaper reporter named Elaine Rowland from Mountain View Voice[20] newspaper, to quickly catch on to Julie's recipe for customer loyalty.

Here is what Elaine had to say in her newspaper review.

*"A long time ago in a galaxy far, far away, it seems restaurants cared about their customers. Back then, customers were welcomed cheerfully and service was every bit as important as the food.*

*Somehow this concept has become alien to many dining establishments.*

*It's rare enough that on encountering great service you look across at your companion and say, 'Wow, they really look after you here.'*

*That's what happened to me on my first visit to the Village Pantry. Co-owner Julie Ogilvy estimates that a whopping 85% of the Pantry's weekday customers are regulars.*

*It is an amazing number and easy to believe after hearing her call across the counter to customers by name, asking if they need refills on their coffee.*

*I looked for a hidden camera when a customer at the next table said Julie makes **everyone** feel special here.*

*Someone at another table responded with, 'That's why my kids love coming here. Julie even told me to go ahead and eat. She would cut up the pancakes for the kids.'*

*The adoration between Julie and the customers is remarkable.*

*And—**the food is great too**."*

---

20. Restaurant Review, *Village Pantry,* by Elaine Rowland, Mountain View Voice, April, 2008

# 5 From Sales to Shelters

### *God Bless Those Who Care* from a Sales VP

Turning personnel loose with that *You take the risk; I'll take the blame* philosophy really showed dividends during one almost disastrous situation at Grid Systems where I had recently become the national customer service manager.

The sales organization in Chicago was in a duel with our strongest competitor to sell many laptop computers to a major Midwest manufacturer. The sales demonstration to the customer was scheduled on a Tuesday, with the competition to show off their new products on Thursday—to an audience of twelve of the company's senior management and sales personnel.

Tuesday at midday a frantic call came in to our West Coast support operation. "You've got to help. Six of the twelve laptop computers we were demonstrating did not work. We did not have time to fully analyze what happened. We *have to* have replacements by tomorrow. The customer has agreed to give us another chance."

I rallied our team together for the challenge. We did not have even two units available as replacements. That's when the dedication and commitment of our team—fueled by the trust and caring we had developed during a turnaround situation—quickly moved into action. We went into our *interrupt anyone on behalf of the customer* mode—a philosophy loved by sales and sometimes frustrating to those who did not fully comprehend customer-focused urgency.

One of our service personnel, Bob, knew the ropes of the repair center where he had previously worked. He found two computers in the process of being repaired and *goaded* his buddies into dropping everything else and fixing these two units first. Bob also spoke to the receiving and shipping area and found that two more units were to arrive that day for refurbishment. Of course, Bob and his new team latched onto these laptops quickly.

One of our administrators had worked in the product development area. She noticed two laptops on the desks of departmental personnel. Not for long. Via some strained conversations we were able to commandeer the two units.

That night at 9 p.m. Bob personally took the six computers to the San Francisco airport for a counter-to-counter delivery to Chicago. At 5 a.m. the Chicago sales support person, Mark, picked up the computers and rushed them to the customer site. He worked tirelessly with his assistant to *bring the 12 computers to life*.

Everyone held their breath as the sales demonstration began. They *all* worked. The customer was amazed. They had never seen this type of responsiveness. They ordered more units than originally planned.

Shortly afterward came the thank you note from Don Paul, the Vice President of sales. "God bless those who care," said a very appreciative sales executive.

The competition—never had a chance of upstaging a *miracle*.

Caring in Action = *teamwork, customers and* ***revenue***.

# Caring—Feelings and the Purchase

The book *Guerrilla Selling*[21] reinforces how feelings really do lead to action and revenue from a sales perspective stating that:

*Guerrillas use emotions to sell to the prospect's unconscious wants and needs. Listen for all your prospect's articulated and undisclosed priorities. Prospects buy on emotions. At the deepest level, all decisions are emotional. We buy to improve our status, to feel good, to avoid pain and to be well thought of in our community. Then we justify the decision with the facts. We tell ourselves and others that we bought because of the specific features and benefits found in the brochures and sales pamphlets.*

*About your own emotions, remember no one can enter your fortress without your permission. You will be told "no" thousands of times. You're the one who must decide if people are going to hurt you personally.*

The examples in *Care: You Have the Power* reinforce that the feelings associated with care very much affect some of the decisions we make.

# The Care Factor and Telemarketing

We have probably all had the experience of receiving a phone call from a *telemarketing robot* who was unable to build any personal connection with us on the telephone.

When done correctly, the *care factor* can have a very positive effect on telephone relationships. *Telemarketing Magazine*[22] published a survey noting what customers most appreciated when they received a solicitation phone call of some type.

---

21. Bill Gallagher, Orvel Ray Wilson and Jay Levinson, *Guerrilla Selling* (Houghton Mifflin, 1992)
22. General Survey, *What is Attractive to the Telemarketing Customer*, Telemarketing, October, 1999

The results came out as:

- 51% Enthusiasm

- 25% Empathy

- 10% Manners and charm

- 7% Product knowledge

- 5% Company name

- 2% Other

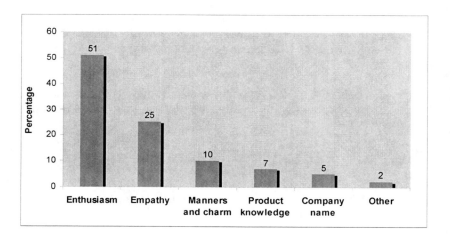

My perspective on the above information is that 86% (enthusiasm, empathy and manners and charm) revolves around having a successful relationship.

## *No* can be a Positive—if You *Care*

Lori Laub paved the way for exceptional service in a *caring* environment in positions as Vice President of Customer Service for both Great Plains Software and Intuit Corporation.

Great Plains, based in Fargo, North Dakota, went on to win many national awards including the highest level of service accolade—the *Grand National* from INC Magazine.

While Lori was showing off her enthusiastic organization at Intuit she commented to me that, "Even if the answer to a customer request is *no* I want them to feel better than when they contacted us in the first place. I want them to realize that we do care about them and want them to be successful."

Obviously that philosophy worked in those companies given the ongoing growth of their customer base. The many awards Lori's organizations received demonstrated her ability to implement a *leadership is caring in action* philosophy. Once again, *both* her personnel and the customers were the beneficiaries.

Yes, *caring* can definitely contribute to bottom line success.

# Caring and Followup—a Great Way to Sell More

Jean Mork Bredeson decided to use her years of experience—and commitment to success with customers—to build her own organization and named it *Service 800*.

She found a niche working with well-known computer and retail companies to provide active followup to their customers regarding a variety of sales and service situations.

Many times Jean's representatives—when dealing with major clients—would hear comments like, "You're the only ones who called us back. We will definitely do our future purchasing with you."

The philosophy has worked extremely well for Service 800 and their customers. The company has expanded from its base in Minneapolis, Minnesota, to having offices internationally in London and Shanghai and now using 30 languages to communicate with customers.

Complicated? Of course not. The customers got that good feeling that *someone cared.*

# The Janitor Cares—and we sell more because of him

Jerry Rosen, Vice President of a manufacturing company in New York can't help smiling when he relates the story of Hank, the maintenance person in their corporate facility.

Says Jerry, "Hank empties the trash baskets and sweeps the floors. We have been told by several customers that he is the *best sales person* at our facility. Whenever we take clients or potential customers on a plant tour, we introduce them to Hank as we pass by."

"When customers meet Hank they are always impressed by his very positive attitude and comment to us about it. We have been told that if the janitor feels that good about the place, we must be doing something—maybe a lot of things—right. We try to impress on each of our employees that they are also salespeople in the eyes of the customer."

Obviously, Hank cared a lot about his job. He heard the message. One might say that he created the message.

# Do the Customers Feel Cared for? Find Out!

How do you want customers to feel after they have had contact with you or your organization—either in person or over the phone or via e-mail? What do you want them to say about their experience with you? How do you want them to describe their experience?

Will the customer say that you cared about them?

Three simple questions—suggested by Jim Steffen, a service authority, can bring forth extremely useful information which creates opportunities for further action.

Try asking these three questions of your personnel:

- How do you want people to feel after having contact with you?

- What do you want them to say about you?

- How do you want them to describe their experience with you?

It is imperative that the responses to these questions be in writing. Information will be more thought out than that of a verbal response.

Without exception, there will be some new and creative ideas.

# Service and Caring Equalled $$ Here

As I managed the customer resource center at Grid Systems through a turnaround situation to become more focused on customers, sales finally trusted us enough to send a prospective major account customer to view what we might do for his organization.

A major component of our turnaround had been my personal caring philosophy—geared to ensure we could create a winning situation for each of our personnel. My statements to the group had included:

**You take the risk; I'll take the blame.**

Of course those words sound good; however without the type of caring that built trust they would have been meaningless. I knew our employees had to see my words in action—and they did over time.

I decided to meet personally with Walt Gasparovic, our potential customer who was a Vice President at Baxter International. It was my belief that Walt should view our personnel in action—showing off what an environment highlighted by *caring* might produce in terms of customer satisfaction.

I stood in front of the service organization, highlighted by a central group with low walls between them. They took the first-line calls and e-mails from customers and sometimes had significant interactions with each other.

As I spoke with Walt, he appeared uninterested in what I had to say—usually looking away and not appearing to hear much of what I had to say. I just *knew* I had personally blown the opportunity given to us by sales.

When I finished, Walt looked at me and said, "*What* are you doing here? I've *never* seen such enthusiasm by people working on customer problems all day. Perhaps you could even help our own organization."[23]

Walt truly understood the Baxter philosophy: We win if our customers win. Walt now runs his own service company. Did it work? Walt signed a contract for significant numbers of laptop computers for his organization. *Feeling care in the air* really works. The lessons for me:

- Understand what your people need, individually and collectively.

- Ensure they have the tools they need to succeed.

- Always show you care about each person individually.

- Who benefits? Employees—and they pass out the caring to customers.

# Mary Kay Ash and the Caring Values

In his book *More Than a Pink Cadillac*[24] Jim Underwood expanded on the values instituted by Mary Kay Ash in building her exceptional organization of distributors.

*Mary Kay believed the only way to maximize profits was to maximize people. Unless you are focused on seeking the best for others, beginning with your own people, you cannot be successful.*

---

23. http://gasparovic.com
24. Jim Underwood, *More Than a Pink Cadillac* (McGraw-Hill, 2003)

*In the early years of the company, she fought a lot of battles with investment bankers and others over this issue. They argued for increased emphasis on the bottom line; she argued for investing in people. And on that score she never gave in.*

The nine keys to success at Mary Kay were:

- Create and maintain a common bond

- Shape the future (think and act strategically)

- Make me feel important (value people)

- Motivate others with recognition and celebration

- Never leave your values

- Innovate or evaporate

- Foster a balance of work and family

- Have a higher purpose

- Be great

*"Make me feel important"* applied to employees and customers.

The Mary Kay organization via its results truly demonstrated the power of caring.

# The Survival Job or Perhaps the Dream Job

It seemed like another nice session of doing business with some wonderful people in recovery at City Team Ministries—people now headed into their job search/career building phase.

Up to the front of the room came Dan when he was called upon.

"What job would you like to have?" I asked Dan.

"I want to be a truck driver," was the reply—somewhat less than enthusiastic.

My intuition said there was more so we proceeded with the session in front of about 25 men in their phase of the recovery process. Dan and I spoke some more.

Then Dan blurted out, "Do you know what I *really* want?"

"No, I don't," I replied with some surprise at the extent of Dan's emotion.

"I really want to open a Mexican restaurant. I want to hire youth so they can work there and avoid the pitfalls of the drug and alcohol abuse I went through."

I was touched by Dan's emotion and desire to give back despite his own difficult circumstances. It was evident that others in the room had similar reactions.

There we have a common scenario—what we *have* to do vs. what we *want* to do. Dan was comfortable enough to share his real dream in life.

What made Dan feel safe enough to speak up and tell us the real truth about what he wanted? Said Dan, "I got the feeling that you and the others in the room really *cared* about what I wanted. I trusted you."

Once again we have the *care equation*. When we listen—and listen attentively—people do feel our caring manner and trust develops.

## Moving Out of the Shelter—with a Little Care

One of the more complex challenges I encountered was when working with parents at the San Jose Family Shelter. While the work and seminars centered around creating employment opportunities, I found the real opportunity often was in ensuring that participants rebuilt their confidence in a way that would assist in effectively marketing themselves to potential employers.

Although they had been through difficult times, I found the participants to generally be very positive.

Mary—a former national journalist—and her husband—who spoke limited English—had been in the shelter several weeks with their baby. She encouraged me to be a little pushy if that would assist her husband. That's what I did—with care, using my limited Spanish to connect. Mary sent me the following note a few days later:

*The donation of your time and expertise really did help us, Ivan. The worksheet you gave to my husband to prep him for the sessions helped in more than just the obvious ways. The way you played dentist—intruding with questions that showed you care—helped him remember that he had a perfect and beautiful smile. You just helped him to remember his smile—and polished it up a bit.*

*You helped an immigrant with working English feel more confident about approaching a potential employer. You took the time to work on a handshake; you typed a resume for him, in English, with him by your side—both of you working with what passing knowledge you had of each other's language to come up with something positive, tangible and professional to represent his potential and experience.*

*My husband was employed with a full-time job two days after you worked together at the front of the room where everyone could be inspired by the progress. It really made a difference in the way he saw himself.*

*You have a talent for helping people see the value in the work that they've done in life—from fast-food to nationally acclaimed reporting, you help people see and understand that nothing they've done is a throwaway skill or experience—It is all transferable. People who are homeless and working towards permanent housing—like myself—for whatever reason, need exactly the kind of focus and care that you inherently provide along with your professional expertise.*

**I ask myself in this homeless situation—who was training who to learn the importance of caring in life? I was the learner—and lucky to have the opportunity.**

# Military Veteran—from Shelter to Service Star

In 2008, I was assisting in gaining employment for military veterans who had been housed in a homeless shelter on the grounds of the Veterans Administration in Menlo Park, California.

Although many of the candidates had prior experience in a variety of settings and had worked in interim assignments within the hospital system for the past year, the prospects of finding a permanent position outside of the VA system were especially challenging, especially given the competition and the downturn in the economy.

We really needed an employer who would understand the value of *caring* for Marlin, a veteran with one glass eye and difficulty in hearing. He also has a wonderful attitude and is willing to work hard.

Where did I turn to for Marlin? Whole Foods, Palo Alto, California which is noted in Chapter 10 for their service orientation. I knew one of their managers, Phil Lonardo, to be very active and supportive in community efforts. When Phil mentioned to me that he had an opening for a *cart collector and service person* I spoke with Marlin and he rushed over to interview on his bicycle—wearing bicycle gear.

There were many qualified candidates for this position. However, Marlin passed the interview phase with several managers. Two weeks later I noticed an older gentleman almost racing through the parking lot in hot weather collecting carts and assisting customers.

Who else could it be but Marlin? He quickly won the new employee of the month award for his proactive efforts and teamwork and then achieved a personal dream. He bought a new motorcycle. Many other organizations would have been reluctant to give Marlin a chance.

The Whole Foods caring philosophy creates many winners—the company, the employee and, of course, the loyal customers.

Marlin was promoted and is now a cashier on the front line.

# A Lady Veteran—Homelessness to a *Miracle*

Terri was another veteran from Menlo Park, someone who had also had responsible positions working for the federal government, and was now working her way out of a transitional homeless situation.

When we met I was impressed with her positive attitude and questioned her lack of smiling. "Some of my left teeth are missing," said Terri, somewhat embarrassed.

Terri was very willing to do anything viable. However, I saw much more for her and—as with many people in the situation—her confidence needed some rebuilding.

She was offered a position as a housekeeper in a senior citizens' home. However, I saw so much more for Terri. We met again and she excitedly pulled some certificates from her folder of papers. Terri had a passion for working with senior citizens and had volunteered in many programs around the Veterans Administration as an assistant—sometimes also initiating programs.

I saw an ad for an *Activities Coordinator* at another senior citizen center and said to Terri, "That's *you*." In the interim Terri had also gained a full set of teeth and her smile was infectious.

She interviewed and the center wanted *more experience*. We persisted and the week before Easter in 2007—perhaps out of desperation—Terri was given the position. What an incredible match it turned out to be! The senior citizens gravitated to Terri and the activities. Sometimes she was even the bus driver. She assisted with games and added new programs to keep participants occupied.

The next *miracle* happened after a year. Terri achieved her dream of returning to the Veterans Administration as an assistant in the physical therapy rehabilitation department where she believed her skills would be very useful to veterans ranging from World War II to those returning from Iraq with physical ailments.

She's in her early 50s and had just finished doing 16 laps in the pool so she could also be a lifeguard. "The last time I did that I was in my 20s," said a proud Terri.

When you visit the physical therapy area you can see Terri working to assist veterans in many areas, from strength and cardio exercises to therapy in the water. She also works to help build major events to invite the participation of the veterans.

Homeless no more is Terri. Lucky are her many clients, yet Terri feels the luckiest of all. She certainly felt cared for by those who gave her another chance.

# 6 | *Care*: The Foundation of Trust

## The Need for Appreciation

William James, known as the father of American psychology had this to say:

**The deepest need of human beings is the need to feel appreciated.**

How better to do it than by applying a little *care* to the interactions we have with others.

## Bill Campbell: Football Coach to Intuit Chairman

Bill Campbell (also known as *coach*) has had a storied career—going from football coach at Columbia University to Executive Vice President of Sales and Marketing during the early growth at Apple Computer to President and Chairman of the Board of Intuit Corporation.

His words on *trust* are simple:

*More trust equals more motivation and participation. I've tried it. It works.*

Bill has more than tried it. He has lived it and the results have been demonstrated.

When I asked a customer service supervisor at Intuit what he liked about the company, he said, "The president shows he *cares* about us. Bill Campbell got on the phones right next to me and took calls from the customers." That also showed customers that senior management cared about them too.

While many senior executives may purport to not have the time to spend taking incoming customer calls as Bill did, there is also a fear factor. Management may be concerned that their people will find out they don't know all the answers.

Once again, people are not looking for what you know necessarily; they do want to know that you care. The actions needed are small in nature and tremendous in terms of their impact.

# Trust is the Glue

Warren Bennis co-authored the book *Leaders*[25] with Burt Nanus. They state that true leaders have an uncanny way of enrolling people in their vision through their optimism—sometimes unwarranted optimism. For them the glass is not half full; it's brimming.

They believe—as all exemplary leaders they have studied—that they can change the world or, at the very least, make a dent in the universe. They're all purveyors of hope.

Confucius said that leaders are *dealers in hope.*

**Trust** is the lubrication that makes it possible for organizations to work. Trust implies *accountability*, predictability and reliability. It's what sells products and keeps organizations humming. Trust is the glue that maintains organizational integrity.

---

25. Warren Bennis and Burt Nanus, *Leaders* (Harper Business, Feb. 1997)

Chapter 6: Care: The Foundation of Trust

**Positive self-regard** is the ability to accept people as they are. It's the:

- Capability to understand what people are like on their terms, rather than judging them.

- Capacity to approach relationships and problems in terms of the present rather than the past.

- Ability to treat those close to you with the same courteous attention that you extend to strangers and casual acquaintances.

- Ability to trust others, even if the risk seems great.

- Ability to do without constant approval and recognition from others.

A large part of the leader's job is to take risks. Risking cannot be pleasing to everyone.

Employees in those environments were willing to take a chance because they felt they were a part of something magical and they wanted to work that extra hour or make that extra call.

Once again, the *caring foundation* pays off in many ways.

# The Suggestion Box—the Action is *Now*

Rick LeBlanc is another caring senior executive who works diligently to ensure there is open communication between his employees and himself. He shows by his *actions* that ideas are encouraged and listened to. Rick does not want filters—human resources or anyone else—to affect his direct relationship with personnel throughout the company.

The *Suggestion Box* often sits in hallways of organizations, rarely utilized since employees have found via past contributions that their ideas are rarely acknowledged—and certainly not acted upon.

Rick takes a different view with *his* suggestion box. It sits in front of the company cafeteria. The empty suggestion forms often have to be refilled because of their heavy usage.

What does Rick do?

At the monthly company meeting he personally unlocks the box and reads each suggestion himself to the attendees. Rick is able to commit to immediate action to some of the suggestions. For others, he offers appropriate research and, hopefully, resolution.

Rick says that, "People respect that the president is brave enough to read the suggestions aloud and in public."

Either Rick or a member of his direct team follows up with each contributor to thank them for their ideas and personally encourages them to continue to give their feedback.

Employees know that if something is *too* sensitive they can go directly to Rick with their concerns—and they do.

What do employees know about Rick? **He's a leader who cares and takes action.**

# Nordstrom Sets the *Golden Rule of Retail Care and Trust*

We are familiar with the golden rule: "Do unto others as you would have them do unto you." However, Nordstrom has taken *care* to the next level. Their rule for sales associates in dealing with customers is blatantly simple:

**Rule # 1** Use your good judgment at all times. There will be no additional rules.

They also add that their number one goal is to provide outstanding customer service. Nordstrom encourages employees to set both their personal and professional goals high. Says a Nordstrom Vice President, "We have great confidence in our employees' ability to achieve their goals. We also know that if our employees see that we care about their personal well-being they will pass that philosophy on to the customers."

A key for Nordstrom for utilizing their *Golden Rule* is in hiring people with the positive attitude to carry out their philosophy in dealing with customers.

# A Venture Capitalist Who Understands the *Care* Equation

Bill Davidow, a venture capitalist who founded MDV, Mohr Davidow Ventures in Menlo Park, California, authored *Total Customer Service*[26] before many of the fad programs began to come and go.

His advice on the *caring factor* and its relationship to employees, customers and revenue is simple and straightforward: Says Bill,

*"The companies that lead in customer service pay extraordinary attention to their employees. They show that they care via their programs of support."*

# Thank You Mr. CEO—*for What?*

As president of UpShot, a customer relationship management company based in Northern California, Keith Raffel always believed in spending a significant amount of his time amongst his people—not pigeonholed in an elaborate office.

Keith did not utilize a senior human resources person—not wanting to do what many companies do—having someone deflect communication and creative ideas, which should go directly to a leader of an operation.

His style must have been working. During one of the hectic downturns in Silicon Valley, Keith said he was walking to his office and was approached by one of his sales support personnel.

"Thank you Keith," said the young lady.

"For what?" asked Keith, wondering what was on his employee's mind.

---

26. William H. Davidow and Bro Uttal, *Total Customer Service* (Harper and Row, 1989)

"For my having a job. I really appreciate how hard you have worked for us and for the company."

Any wonder that Keith's employees were inspired? Always include *caring* in any recipe with people.

Keith also believed in the importance of the development of his people—both inside and outside of their jobs. He lived that philosophy himself, becoming the successful author of *Dot Dead* while running a company and raising four children.

# Using *Care* to Dispose of *Fear* (the Single Mom)

A significant fraction of our workforce is composed of single moms or dads who are sometimes faced with the dilemma of maintaining work as a priority when family situations call for their presence.

During my early days as manager of an internal customer support function at Apple Computer, I was speaking with one of our representatives, Susan, and asked how her children were doing.

Susan had two sons and responded that the younger one, age 7, was home sick. When I inquired as to who was with him, she responded with, "Oh, he's OK for a few hours. I call him and he has my number."

I knew that Susan had been under a lot of pressure, having been sick herself for a few days. I immediately presumed that she must be fearful of losing her job if she missed any more work.

I asked Susan if she had any concerns about her employment and she hesitated—leading me to make an immediate response. I said, "Susan the only way you will lose your job in my organization is if you don't go home and be with your son. We can take care of the situation here. After all, we are a team and we should be *caring* about each other in times of need."

Susan breathed a sigh of relief and said, "Oh, really? That's wonderful. I really appreciate your support."

Although Susan was already respected by her customers in providing them support, her morale rose to a higher level after this incident.

As always, a little *caring and personalized support to employees* goes a long way toward enhancing productivity, loyalty and retention. It builds that trusting foundation.

Susan's attendance record after that was pretty much impeccable—and there were no children home alone.

I want to add that sometimes we have to avoid some of the corporate policies and do what is best for ourselves and our team.

# At the Root of Quality and Caring

James Autry, former President of the Meredith Magazine Group and author of many books including *Life and Work: A Manager's Search for Meaning*[27] and *Love and Profit: The Art of Caring Leadership*[28] describes the need for a *trusting* foundation in order to be successful in building quality-oriented business environments.

He notes that employees need an environment in which they can integrate their work and their lives in ways that provide meaning and fulfillment of dignity and worth. This type of setting can be conducive to people achieving the impossible.

Movements like TQM (Total Quality Management) are often turned into quick fix-it systems, rather than bringing about fundamental change in the social architecture or culture of the workplace.

Fear can set in and people at the grass roots level will be hesitant to innovate if they are worried about their jobs. They will be scared to do anything new.

---

27. James Autry, *Life and Work: A Manager's Search for Meaning* (Quill, 1995)
28. James Autry, *Love and Profit: The Art of Caring Leadership* (Harper, 1992)

I must add that my personal experience as Director of Quality/Customer Care for JBL International confirms what James Autry says. TQM was brought in, there was a plethora of meetings and soon TQM was sent on its way.

As with the other examples of success in *Care: You Have the Power*, it is imperative that leaders show that they care and can build a trusting foundation. Leaders should show themselves as *servants*, a resource—not a boss.

# Caring and Trust—the Levi's Way in Europe

Pete Thigpen teaches ethics at the Haas Business School at the University of Berkeley and works with business executives and their dreams of success at the renowned Aspen Institute in Colorado.

In Pete's prior role as President of Levi Strauss Europe, he faced many challenges in working with a demanding network of distributors during a hectic growth period for the multinational company.

His logistics and operations team let Pete know about the quagmire of paperwork they faced in dealing with many customer return policies and operational issues associated with supporting the distributor network from many countries. There were many issues which led to a significant amount of frustration where the *now* is critical.

Pete is someone who truly cares about both his own employees and customer relationships. His solution in one key area was swift and quickly established more trusting relationships with his distributors. Pete's dictate:

*We will begin trusting our distributors since they are our front-line. I don't want to penalize 97% of them for the 3% who may take advantage of our policies. I want to show our distributors that we are listening to them and that we are taking proactive steps to show that we care about their success.*

Processes and policies were refocused toward *trust* and this established the quicker throughput necessary to return products and ensure they were replaced quickly when necessary.

The trusting policies enhanced customer relationships and also increased—rather than decreased—revenue to the company.

Pete took that philosophy and has utilized *trust* throughout his career.

# Big Brother is not Watching Over Here

I'm a regular customer at the Palo Alto Café. It's easily notable that owner Keyvan Alikermanshahi seems to continually have a very motivated staff of servers and other personnel.

I mentioned to Keyvan that it had been difficult to feel trusted when I worked in retail because of the overhead cameras focused on me at the cash register.

Keyvan replied, "I trust my people, not the cameras. That's why I don't have them here."

It is also notable in my research that when the internal environment is one of trust then employee theft actually goes down.

# Destroying Trust—in an instant with a non-caring moment

After the closure of one of my companies, Myteam.com, one of our super-star performers, Manda, took on a support role at an international company in San Francisco. The company, based in Europe—where they purported to have offices characterized by high morale and productivity—called me in to discuss the low morale in their local office.

The organization had been through four managers in the past two years; therefore, *change* was the first suspect.

However, I quickly learned from Manda that the customer service representatives were all dedicated people—and were frustrated by the processes which seemed to inhibit their ability to give optimal care to customers. Manda, whose first corporate role had been in my organization—where she enthusiastically supported Little League—quickly grasped the difference between our proactive support and reactive service.

While the San Francisco company was weighing whether to do some type of employee survey—in which I personally always place little credence—Manda confidentially let me know what the core issue really was.

The representatives had met with their new senior management and Manda had encouraged everyone to speak the truth so that management could address and resolve the issues. The other personnel heeded Manda and spoke up with their concerns and potential solutions. *All* related to building a healthier environment that would enhance the customer focus of the organization.

The *non-caring* response from senior management, "If you don't like it here, why don't you leave?"

No wonder the statistic noted in *Driving Fear Out of the Workplace* that 7 of 10 employees stop speaking up with their ideas. In that instant positive morale died—forever under that management structure. Unfortunately, it is very typical of what happens when non-listening is the response to people who lead with their hearts—in any scenario.

I could only smile when management expressed their concerns about morale in their United States branch.

# Caring and the Trust Factor

In their book, *Reinventing Leadership*[29] Warren Bennis and Robert Townsend hit the nail on the head regarding *trust*. Here is what they said:

---

29. Warren Bennis and Robert Townsend, *Reinventing Leadership* (W.H. Morrow, 1995)

*Trust*: You can't direct people to trust you.
It starts with consistent action, including trusting
people below you though they meet only 50
per cent of your expectations.

You've got to really *convince* yourself they
are capable of growing the other 50 per cent.
Eventually you will be trusted if your actions
are the same as your words.

Trust is the emotional glue. It's interactive;
there's no such thing as *instant trust*.
Trust also includes *caring as the foundation.*
**Really caring** about the fate of others—being
on their side.

**Peter Drucker, management guru:**

*Most of what we call management consists of making it difficult for
people to get their work done.*[30]

# Caring, Trust and a New Team at Apple

I certainly had not learned that caring was the foundation of trust and
that trust breeds success from any educational program when I
wrestled with the dilemma of how to turn a skeptical support organization into a dynamic team in the earlier days at Apple Computer.

As the customer service manager I had worked with our support team
to significantly improve our customer relationships. It worked well
enough that the organization decided to merge another support group
into ours.

"Oh no, here we go again. People are demoralized and overworked," I
said to myself. We had to quickly build trust so I set up a meeting of the
groups, also inviting my boss and his direct superior, the Vice President
of the area.

---

30. http://brainyquote.com/quotes/authors/p/peter_f_drucker.html

The stage was set. All 26 of us fit around an oblong table in the conference room. I realized that some of the participants had complained on more than one occasion about their workload—without seeing the type of action that would resolve their frustration.

I thought, "What can I do differently?" and a light bulb went on in my head. I said we were going to go around the room and each person would contribute something positive about working in the organization. This was received with much dismay—since many participants wanted me to hear how bad the situation was.

We progressed around the room and soon had 26 positives on the wall that at least made people think a little differently about the conditions.

*Now*, it was time to go around the room and invite 26 negatives—the opportunities as far as I was concerned. Ironically, there were five requests which could be dealt with immediately. I committed to having those five situations taken care of the next week—with regular feedback on the remaining opportunities. One was as simple as moving a copy machine down the hall.

One week later there were five solutions implemented. People began to trust again. ***They just wanted to know that someone cared enough to listen to their input and would take action***. That's pretty much the opportunity all around us. ***Show care and take action***. There must be enough trust to motivate people to share ideas through their own fears and concerns.

# Care and Trust While Terrified of Swimming

Melon Dash has accomplished what others would call *miracles* with many people who were terrified of ever learning to swim. Her organization, The Miracle Swimming Institute, has worked throughout the United States and internationally with people who thought they would never be able to swim.

One of Melon's clients had been in the United States Navy for four years and somehow escaped the attention of any superior who might think he should be able to swim.

Melon might be called a *goddess of caring*. She builds trust quickly in a way that many of her clients—who have sometimes never been in a pool or were scared at an early age—work their way back into the water.

Says Melon, "Trust is the currency. If you break trust, there is no currency. And you don't get it back. People won't risk and spend unless they trust."

"My clients are fearful at first. When they experience how safe it is and how much I personally care about their well-being, they begin to trust. I listen to their concerns and fears, answer their questions and consider their feelings about being in the water. If it's not fun we don't go on to the next step."

Given her results and national recognition, Melon's clients have obviously learned that she cares about them and their courage comes out.

I know it's true. I took Melon's course.

# Building Trust: Care is the Foundation

In their book *Built on Trust*,[31] Tom Steding and Arky Ciancutti use their many years of experience with corporations to make the message blatantly clear.

*The principal behind the leadership organization, with its non-connected teams, is that people have a natural inclination to give. In fact, we have found in our combined 50 years of working with people that everyone has a passionate desire to contribute. They do care about what is happening around them. We have a hunger to be part of something bigger than ourselves, especially when that something bigger reflects and amplifies our inherent values. This desire is a primary emotional need at work—and it must be satisfied if we are to be productive and happy in our jobs.*

---

31. Tom Steding and Arky Ciancutti, *Built on Trust* (McGraw-Hill, 2000)

Tom and Arky add:

> If you genuinely **care** about people, authentically want
> their input, live by the Trust Model guidelines and give
> people the information and training they need to live
> these guidelines themselves, then you are doing everything
> you can to create a culture of trust that benefits
> everyone in the organization.

> With customers, the listening and **caring** is what
> creates the initial closure. The result is an energy flow
> from the customers to the company. Likewise with employees.

> The new leaders are self-aware and genuinely involved with
> their teams on more than superficial levels. They know
> how to create environments in which people can make
> the contributions they want to make and be as productive
> as they can be.

> The new leaders truly **care**.

# Act—Creating that Caring Environment in Business

The *act* principles that I developed and followed in building customer care organizations worldwide encompass the principles in *Care: You Have the Power.*

**A** - Hire a positive **attitude**, particularly when recruiting individuals who will be working directly with customers. Stew Leonard, president and CEO of a grocery store chain that has received worldwide acclaim for excellence in customer service and quality, says he hires only one out of every 16 people he interviews. Trust your intuition too and be willing to take the extra time to find the right person for the team and the customers.

**C** - Find people with **conation**. John McCormack, author of *Self Made in America: Plain Talk for Plain People About the Meaning of Success,* points out that the current criteria most companies use for recruiting doesn't measure conation, which he calls "the will to succeed, the quest for success, that attitude which says: to stop me, you'll have to knock me down." Employees with conation will want to grow and develop; they will also take the extra step on behalf of their teammates and customers.

**T - Trust, training, tools, teamwork** and **thank you**. Following are some of the ways to put these five areas into play in the organization:

- Ask each person for any areas in which he or she would like to grow. Find a creative way to ensure that this is at least a small component of the job. By **showing that you** *care* and helping employees prepare for their next step your staff will quickly learn to **trust** you.

- Ensure each person receives the **training** they need to support their focus on getting the job done—or with customers. Trust employees to make the right decisions and allow them to learn from their mistakes.

- **Tools** can include technologies and processes. Ensure there are no barriers to employee success particularly in direct relationships with customers.

- **Teamwork** is critical. Do not compromise in this area. A group that works well together is an inspiration to each other.

- **Thank you**. Say it often—and publicly.

# Chapter 7

# Care and Recruiting

**Hal Rosenbluth and $5 Billion Says Care Works**

## Caring Must be in Their Nature

Hal Rosenbluth led his company, Rosenbluth Travel, from a $20 million business to $5 billion in revenue before selling the company to American Express in 2003. He is now Chairman of Take Care Health Systems.

In his book *The Customer Comes Second,* Hal said part of his success in building the company was *looking for nice people. What is in someone's heart cannot be discovered in a resume. Caring must be inherent in their nature.*

Hal added that in the employee selection process, *kindness, caring, compassion and un-selfishness carry more weight than years on the job, impressive salary history and stacks of degrees.*

Joel Peterson is Founder of the highly successful Peterson Partners, a private equity investment firm based in Salt Lake City. He also teaches courses in entrepreneurship and leadership at Stanford University's Graduate School of Business.

Joel's advice on building trust: **Become everyone's assistant. Show that you care enough to relate to the importance of *all* positions in the organization.**

Joel adds, "We look for brains and heart in our business. We need people who care. When I was with Trammell Crow, we generally hired people from outside the real estate industry."

# What a Difference when Dee Dee Got the Chance

What an incredible difference it can make when we do not stifle the natural talent and enthusiasm we encounter from people.

I had just taken over as the new customer service manager at Grid Systems—at that time one of the leading suppliers of laptop computers.

The overworked service organization needed a fresh infusion to improve the downward spiraling morale. Although job recruiting fairs are often staffed by the human resource personnel, I also manned the booth in Santa Clara, California, so I could see potential applicants. I also knew I could not measure *attitude and enthusiasm* from looking at an applicant's resume.

A young lady named Dee Dee rushed up to our booth—very passionately claiming, "This looks interesting; however, I don't have experience in high-technology."

Dee Dee's refreshing attitude seemed like the perfect antidote for our organization. I put her resume in my pocket to ensure no one could rule her out because of lack of experience. I was later to find out that Dee Dee trained personnel at hotels on how to use their computers. She did not yet understand how that translated as a transferable skill to any industry.

I gave Dee Dee the position of Customer Relations Supervisor. Within three months the department was given positive accolades in national computer industry publications. Morale skyrocketed. Dee Dee had taken over a national customer care team which was under siege and quickly turned it into a world-class operation, with the addition of some other new talent.

Where is the young lady with *no relevant experience* now? Dee Dee founded Proactive Business Solutions, a technology consulting company, in Oakland, California, and quickly grew the company into an organization of over 100 personnel.

She earned an advanced degree from the University of California, Berkeley, and won the Oakland Chamber of Commerce award for woman-owned business of the year.

Inc. Magazine came out with their selection of the top 100 inner city-based companies in the United States. Dee Dee and Proactive Business Solutions were already ranked number 40. Once again, a little *caring and risk-taking and believing in the talents of people went a long way.*

# Remove the Educational Shackles Too

When I was hired as the new Customer Service Manager during the early days of Cisco Systems, I was fortunate to work for co-founder Sandy Lerner, who strongly believed in the capabilities of the people in her organization.

Soon afterward, Cyd, one of the first employees in the company, was advised by Sandy to see me about growth opportunities. Sandy apparently told Cyd that I too *believed in the capabilities each person offered.* Cyd had been in charge of purchasing and some manufacturing functions and knew the potential customer base very well.

*However,* Cyd did not have the MBA mandated at that time for a management position in her own manufacturing organization. Thus, her growth opportunities were stunted.

My requirements were different. One of my rules has always been—**Never dismiss a sharp candidate because of educational protocol.**

It was easy to care about Cyd and her desire to further develop herself in the company. I reviewed her wonderful experience and trusted my intuition. I just *knew* that she would be a very capable manager. I asked this talented employee if she would like to manage the repair center. She was dumbfounded and explained that she had no experience in that area which also reported to me.

I said, "Neither do I. We'll just have to figure it out together."

Within three months, Cyd took a very informal department and built it into a model repair operation where international distributors even stopped by to have their pictures taken. She was masterful in convincing engineers to listen to customer feedback passed along from the previously unheeded repair center personnel—no small task in establishing internal organizational credibility.

Where is Cyd today? She has a Ph.D. and has done organizational consulting with companies like American Express while also educating students at the university level.

Heck, what did I do? *Cared enough to take a risk.* I had to look past whatever fear I may have had and believe in people. Cyd did it all, given the opportunity.

# Hal Continues—Recruiting should be an event to remember

Hal Rosenbluth also takes a real-world approach—albeit unconventional—to finding and retaining outstanding personnel. He could be known as *the king of caring* based on the comments from his people.

Says Hal:

*Look for nice people. What is in someone's heart cannot be discovered in a resume. **Caring must be inherent in their nature**.*

*In the selection process, caring, kindness, compassion and unselfishness should carry more weight than years on the job, an impressive salary history and stacks of degrees.*

*The beginning of their career should be an event to remember.*

*The processes must then support the growth and development of new hires.*

*If there is an error rate, it's almost always a sign of unhappiness.*

*Internal unhappiness surfaces before client dissatisfaction.*

*Make trainings fun—use the kindergarten principle to learning.*

*(The kindergarten approach ensures participation.)*

*Processes should be enabling and make things possible. The people executing them are then free to concentrate on the finer points and provide added touches.*

# Great Attitude or Experience? Which do You Want?

Mike Wallau has had a successful career in business, as a chef and now in restaurant management. In fact, Mike's restaurant business expanded during difficult economic times in Silicon Valley.

When you enter one of Mike's restaurants, such as Mike's Café in Palo Alto, you can just *feel* the upbeat attitude of the hostesses, servers, and chefs.

Mike's credo: "You can teach an *inexperienced* person with a smile to care for customers. You just can't teach an *experienced* person without a smile to create that type of positive first impression."

Simple? Another reason to give someone with that positive attitude a chance.

## Some Hallway Advice

When Bill Campbell was Executive Vice President of Sales and Marketing at Apple Computer, he was known for his motivating, vibrant coaching style—presumably carried forth from his days as head football coach at Columbia University.

Bill continually pushed people to be willing to take non-traditional approaches to building great teamwork within his organization.

His advice on recruiting has always been very meaningful and useful to me.

What did Bill say? "Walk the halls in the company and you will find great people. You don't have to go outside the company to find the talent you need."

No wonder Bill engendered such tremendous loyalty. He demonstrated a creative way to show people you *care* about them and are willing to take risks in giving them opportunities to grow and develop themselves.

## Stanford University and How to Succeed in Business by Really *Caring*

Joel Peterson, a successful entrepreneur and investor, teaches real estate investment, leadership and the management of growing enterprises at Stanford University. Historically, his classes are oversubscribed, as so many students want to take advantage of Peterson's knowledge.

Peterson is also known for lecturing on *how to succeed in business by really caring*. He says that success in business isn't worth anything unless you are really happy.

Joel, also a Harvard MBA, talks about being humble and becoming successful by *being everyone's assistant. That is one surefire way to build trust.*

He lived his words in businesses that have included buildings all over the world. *If you stay focused on the objective, the team will help you chart the path.*

He goes against conventional wisdom when recruiting people for the team. *Hire for brains and heart, not experience. At Trammel Crow, we generally hired people from outside the industry. We hired for smarts, high standards and potential.*

**"Make a commitment to someone," says Joel. "Show that you care."**

# Rosa the Geophysicist—Caring is Contagious

I had to move quickly when I took on the role as Director of Customer Care for Myteam.com which was partnered with Little League baseball and its 3 million participants to bring more cohesiveness to the organization via usage of Internet tools.

My boss John told me he had just leased a new e-mail response system. If I did not want to personally run it, then I had better find someone capable of doing that quickly.

As luck would have it, Rosa, a young geophysicist from the University of California, Berkeley, showed up for a job interview. She had a year of experience in service, none of it involved with e-mail systems. I figured that if she could climb mountains, she could figure this task out. I hired her quickly.

Rosa quickly gained the respect of her co-workers and the Little League volunteers with her tenacious, go-getter attitude. There were no *black holes of non-response* when Rosa was involved.

She also built rapport with the sales people. They asked if Rosa might accompany them to a sales convention and I said that would be great. Rosa had no idea what her involvement would be—other than to hang around the sales personnel and act nice to the youth sports volunteers.

At the last minute Rosa was asked to do a presentation following that of sales. The sales talk received the normal *that sounds nice* polite response. Rosa, a master at conveying a caring attitude, let the somewhat concerned audience know that she was personally committed to their success in using a new system involving the Internet.

When her talk ended, almost 50 people in the audience rushed up to Rosa. Was Rosa's talk that great? Perhaps. However, it emphasized to a non-technical audience that they need not be concerned about using a new system—which would even further impose on their volunteer activities for the children. Rosa and her team would be there for them whenever needed.

What did the volunteers want? Simply to know they had a relationship with someone they could trust—someone who personally *cared* about their success.

Rosa quickly used up all of her business cards.

# I Walked the Halls. . .Guess What Happened?

As Atari grew rapidly in its early days I was invited to take on a role managing the manufacturing and distribution operations support team. Although there was the initial excitement of joining the *Pacman crowd*, circumstances began to change. Our organization of 31 people in the Consumer Division seemed too top heavy for my own *get more done with less* philosophy.

With the opening of the new Computer Division, I eagerly drew seven boxes on a piece of paper and somewhat naively approached the new Vice President of Operations, Jim Williamson. After being shown into his office and realizing I should get to the point quickly, I showed Jim my chart and mumbled something about accomplishing the results with seven people, whereas the older division was using 31.

Surprisingly, a month later I was called into Jim's office and given the go-ahead to initiate and manage a new support organization in his division. What did I have to begin with? Not much experience, and a piece of paper with seven boxes on it.

Using the Bill Campbell philosophy of taking to the halls I began asking about potential resources. Someone mentioned I should consider *Carol* in inventory control as a candidate, given her work experience in the company.

Off I trekked to Carol's area. There she sat, studiously eyeing me from behind her desk. I let her know I was forming a new group and queried her about her interest in joining our team. Carol gave me a *Who the heck are you and why are you bothering me?* look. Intuitively, I knew I was talking to a powerhouse of a lady.

A few weeks later Carol had become frustrated enough in her current role to let me know she had some interest in our area. She joined us and quickly demolished any expectations I might have had about her abilities. Carol gave our group instant credibility, product knowledge and positive relationships with several operations with whom she had worked. She was a *no nonsense, get-the-job-done* person. Carol went well beyond *clerking* and quickly took on a role training our new personnel.

When the Computer Division closed its doors two years later, Carol followed me to Apple Computer, helping turn a somewhat demoralized internal support group into a dynamic, proactive, enthusiastic team.

Carol's stock in the company rose quickly.

She built a relationship with the marketing organization and became Apple's on-site product manager based in New Zealand.

Quite a path for the inventory control clerk, seemingly going nowhere at Atari!

When I queried Carol about *the look* she gave me when I initially tried to recruit her, she smiled and said, "I could not believe anyone *cared enough to give me a chance to do something else.*"

Yes, as Bill Campbell says, we should all walk the halls more often.

# Recruiting and the Receptionist

I was very proud of myself. Our organization needed a sharp administrator and junior support person to assist with our customers bringing their automotive products to market with our help at Navigation Technologies.

Tanya had just accepted the position after meeting with myself and the members of our team individually.

I assumed she had been influenced by my usual spiel about a personal commitment to the growth and development of each person in the organization.

I asked Tanya, "What most influenced you to accept the position in our group?"

She quickly responded with, "The receptionist. She was so happy and upbeat."

Another theory shot down.

Well, *caring* was in play and Tanya got a positive feeling. However, it was the receptionist—the real frontline hero who established that solid first impression.

# 8 *Care*: The Risk Factor

## Take Off the Shackles

The philosophy that Hall of Fame quarterback Steve Young shares in Chapter 9 on taking personal responsibility can work well in many venues.

My personal mode for many years has been to give employees in organizations I directed the following marching orders:

**You take the risk; I'll take the blame.**

This only works if trust has been built first. Can you recall how often you have called or visited a company and were told that *the policy does not allow us to do what you want*. Do the employees trust me at first to keep my word about their taking risks? Not based on their previous experiences where mistakes were frowned upon and there was enough blame to go around for everyone.

However, once employees began taking small risks and saw that I was serious, the *customer miracles* grew exponentially. Our front-line did not have the company shackles that often hinder motivation.

Once again, *caring in action* works.

# Care and Risk—They Just Wanted a Chance

When a large group at Agilent (a spinoff from the Hewlett-Packard company) was asked where their success really began, they replied:

*My success began when I was given a chance to do something my experience did not yet qualify me to do. I did not have the experience normally required for the step up I was given. My manager cared about me, believed in me and gave me the chance.*

People want to grow and develop. That's the natural process. Our job is to not inhibit that growth because of our own fears and limitations.

# The Quality Stats Look Good—Oops, forgot the *caring*

An extraordinary effort has gone into many *quality programs* to bring about improved productivity and quality. Many of these such as Quality Circles and TQM (Total Quality Management) were long-term, expensive projects with limited results.

There was often one key item missing—the buy-in of the personnel involved.

When I was Director of Customer Care at a multinational consumer company, we had an issue with the quality of the products being sold in Europe. However, the quality statistics were positive.

As the speakers were returned to the United States for evaluation and the problems were diagnosed, one of the manufacturing workers said that, "We told management about this issue many months ago. They seemed to ignore it and told us not to be concerned."

John Persico, an expert in the quality field, accurately stated that, "All the statistical training in the world is useless if employees fear for their jobs. The *quality chart* becomes perfect when management comes around."

Fear and muted communication can be associated with change in virtually all scenarios. The foundation of trust must be built first, prior to implementing new programs.

## Caring and Change—it Can be Painful

This simple quote which I viewed at the Copenhagen airport years ago exemplifies that we need to stay on our path of change and rewards will come:

**The pain of every change disappears when the benefits of the change are realized.**

Whatever we do within each of our situations to demonstrate caring will be worth the effort.

## This Conductor Cared So Much He was Fired. . .and Then

The following story appeared in the Peninsula Daily News[32] in Northern California:

Jeff Papp, the Caltrain conductor suspended for criticizing the commuter railroad's handling of passengers headed for Pacific Bell Park in San Francisco, got his job back yesterday.

Papp, a Caltrain conductor since 1992, will return to work Monday, Caltrain spokeswoman Jan McGovern said.

"I'm delighted, thrilled and ecstatic," Papp said.

---

32. Peninsula Daily News, April, 2000, page 1

Papp got into hot water when the train from San Jose became over-loaded with baseball fans headed for an open house at the new ballpark.

With a standing-room-only crowd of commuters and baseball fans on board, Papp allegedly made remarks on the train's public address system which were critical of Caltrain management's planning for the crush of passengers.

A passenger on the train who happens to be married to the Caltrain operations director reported Papp and he was suspended for a disciplinary hearing.

Yesterday, Amtrak, which employs Papp, decided to drop the suspension and reinstate the conductor.

After Papp's story was printed in the Daily News, he said he received hundreds of letters from passengers who supported him.

"This whole experience has been overwhelming," said Papp. "I'm looking forward to getting back on the train and doing my job."

Steve Schmidt, a Menlo Park city councilman and a member of the Caltrain board said, "People are glad to know there's a human being running the train instead of someone on automatic."

Yes, and a human being who *cares*.

# 9 *Sports*: So Much is About Care

### Caring is remembered

It's not what you say to someone that will be most remembered; it's how you made them feel that people will most readily recall.

The above comment is very applicable to some of our outstanding sports teams.

- Said Mike Shanahan, coach of the Denver Broncos, after their first Super Bowl victory, when he was accused of pushing his players too hard by some of the media, *When players know you care about them, you can push them harder to excel and they will appreciate it.*

- Jim Tressel, coach of an Ohio State NCAA national college championship football team noted that:

    - *We grew together.*
    - *We learned to care about each other.*
    - *We developed great relationships.*

# Steve Young—A Super Bowl winner demonstrates accountability and caring

Steve Young, the Hall of Fame, Super Bowl-winning quarterback from the San Francisco 49ers often demonstrated what leadership *should be*. When there were problems he took personal responsibility for the results, rather than pointing fingers at others.

After a particularly difficult loss to the Buffalo Bills, during which the 49ers were penalized 22 times, Steve quickly showed what personal accountability means.

Said Steve, "I was the quarterback. I was responsible for the poor play of the team that day." Obviously, Steve himself did not cause all those penalties. It was a *team effort*.

However, what Steve was really saying was that, "Each of us should ask what did I do wrong. What can I do better?" He also stated, "When we take personal responsibility for a negative situation, our teammates can refrain from blaming each other and we can move forward." It's no different in business or personal relationships.

Steve Young's style helped diffuse potential conflicts. The situation was much easier to fix when someone *cared enough* to take responsibility—even for the mistakes that were made by others on the team.

The result in this particular situation? The San Francisco 49ers played almost to perfection the following Sunday, winning the game and not allowing their opponent, the New Orleans Saints, to score a single point.

We might say it was a **caring victory** for the 49ers.

# Little League and *the Truth*

Steve Keener, President of the International Little League Association and its 3 million members, was facing a huge public relations disaster for the organization in 2001.

Says Steve, "We had a very public issue to deal with involving an overage player in the Little League World Series."

(League officials learned that Rolando Paulino had been barred from Little League in Latin America for using overage players. A Little League spokesman said that the violation had been overlooked because of miscommunication. Pitcher Danny Almonte, at age 14 over the age limit, had played for Paulino's All-Star team from the Bronx in New York).

Keener added, "We were faced with many challenges in a short time period, including how to handle the matter and making appropriate decisions about a number of individuals involved."

"The one bit of advice I received from a very good friend and leader was, *Let the truth be your guide*. It was rather simple advice to follow; however, it was the right advice. All of our disciplinary actions were predicated on the truth. Our public statements on the matter were straightforward and truthful. This approach served us well as we worked very hard to maintain the credibility of the world's largest and—in my opinion—the most respected youth sports organization."

The matter was quickly resolved. Contrast this with the distrust that developed a few years later during the Ford/Firestone tire controversy and the public's perception of whether the truth was being told.

Steve truly cared. He told the truth. It worked. The controversy quickly dissolved.

## This Yankee Wanted More Caring

According to a story in the media,[33] *When Andy Pettitte bolted the New York Yankees and their home in the Bronx yesterday, he left the Yankees with a huge hole in the rotation and a bigger one in the club-house.*

"It's a huge loss," former Yankee outfielder Paul O'Neill said, referring to Petitte.

---

33. http://sports.espn.go.com/mlb/news/story?id=1683732

Pettitte's departure was a stunning blow to a team that had won 26 World Series titles.

Sounding wistful at times, the 31-year-old left-hander said the Yankees failed to pursue him aggressively, allowing him to turn his attention to Houston, which wound up signing him for $7.5 million less than the Yankees had offered. Boston had made an offer of $52 million for four years according to one source and Pettitte decided he could not go to the Yankees' rival. With the Houston Astros he felt wanted and he would be closer to his home.

While the Astros were aggressive in their pursuit, the Yankees were unusually passive. New York waited until the last day of its exclusive 15-day window to make an offer.

"I never envisioned myself in a different uniform," Pettitte said. "I thought they would make a serious push to sign me earlier."

Would a little more perceived *caring* and perhaps a phone call earlier in the process have made a difference?

The phone call Andy Pettitte wanted must have been made years later. He returned to the Yankees.

# Do You Care if I Take the $65 million and Leave?

Did basketball star Gilbert Arenas want to leave the Golden State Warriors in 2003 to take the $65 million offer from Washington?

On the radio with local broadcasting personalities Ralph Barbieri and Mark Ibanez, Gilbert said, "I played in the Oakland Summer League. My home is here. I wanted to stay. I went and did talk to other teams. I had not really been recruited before and wanted to see what it felt like."

Chris Cohan had been the Warriors owner for about a year and did not know Arenas well. Arenas noted that, *I wanted to hear from Chris that if I signed the one-year new contract and was injured, he would ensure I was cared for.* (The Warriors did counter with a story from their side of the equation).

Gilbert said, "The owner did not say one word to me."

Gilbert's father felt, "They did not show love."

Should Gilbert have told the owner what he wanted? He was only 21 years old at the time. He did say, "I did not need to have $65 million or more. I wanted to hear from the man in charge, not his assistant."

Might it have been that Gilbert Arenas was simply looking for a *little caring*?

# 10 Care and Loyalty

## Whole Foods—Wow, do they care!

Many years ago my wife Naomi was getting ready to attend a sold-out play in which her daughter Cara had a key role. As Naomi was getting ready to leave, she could not find her tickets—*anywhere*!! Panic began to set in.

I suggested that she go to the play since sometimes tickets become available. She reluctantly agreed that was the best option.

Naomi decided to check with the ticket office, just in case there were tickets. She explained her dilemma to the young lady in the box office.

"Just a minute," responded the theater employee. She returned with a white envelope and handed it to Naomi. "Might this be yours?" she asked. Puzzled at receiving what appeared to be a greeting card, Naomi opened the envelope.

Inside was a personalized card with two tickets to the play enclosed. The note said, "I hope whoever lost these tickets still gets to see the play." Signed by Alli Christian at Whole Foods Market in Palo Alto, California.

I *had* to know what would cause a grocery clerk to take this extra step since many people possibly would have thrown out the tickets, which were apparently laying on the floor—*or* simply put them in the lost and found area. I found Alli at the grocery. She said she had children and was concerned about someone else missing out on a children's play. Alli purchased a card on her own, found the location of the box office and ensured the tickets were sent there.

Is that the norm for service at Whole Foods? Next came my call to John Mackey, Chairman of the company, based in Austin, Texas. I managed to get through to John who wondered who this mystery person could be. I explained how impressed I was with the customer care in his organization, gave John the details about the tickets and asked, "What are you doing that causes such a response from your people?"

John paused for a moment and then responded with a statement indicating that he loves and cares for his people.

Yes, John loves his employees. They know he *cares*. So does Naomi. The show was great.

# The Customer Comes Second—Just Ask Hal Rosenbluth

Some businesses define *spirit* as embodying the values of honesty, integrity and high-quality work. Webster's dictionary defines it as: "The vital principle or animating force believed to be within living beings."

*Animating force* can be interpreted as the desire to grow.

Hal Rosenbluth, who built Rosenbluth Travel into a $5 billion company, certainly ascribes to this definition.

Says Hal, "When people and ideas are guarded, their growth is stunted."

The Human Factors Organization in California agrees. When I participated in one of their seminars, the trainer compared the *human biological system* to the *organizational biological system*.

In either case, when natural growth is not supported and nurtured, disease can set in. Such is the state of so many of our organizations where fear and other factors have stunted the desire of employees to grow and contribute.

Hal focuses very much on the processes that create internal customer satisfaction and implements operational efficiencies in a way that the results translate into customer satisfaction and loyalty. Adds Hal:

*The origin of a lack of motivation is a lack of happiness in the workplace. Profits are a natural extension of happiness in the workplace. Our true competitive measure is our **people**.*

Unhappiness surfaces internally before there is client dissatisfaction.

Cross-pollination has brought us some of the most spectacular varieties of plants and flowers known to the world. The same works with people when you give them opportunities to develop themselves.

After all, when was the last time you excelled at something you disliked?

Hal's **people** excel at what they like. A little caring *can* equal a lot of revenue.

Add the words of Milton Chang, a California CEO and venture capitalist who has successfully built many companies.

Milton believes strongly that we must *trust people implicitly until proven untrustworthy. It has really worked for me. People don't want to let other people down, so they perform to their maximum to make themselves deserving of that trust. It is a wondrously positive cycle.*

# Building Loyalty—Simply

The principles that James Autry describes worked extremely well for me in the role as Director of Customer Care at Myteam, a dotcom company which worked with Little League and other youth sports organizations.

Building an environment of employee loyalty and retention relies on a foundation of trust, caring and personalizing relationships when possible. Some of the opportunities which present themselves can have simple solutions.

Mike, one of our customer support representatives, sheepishly came to me with a request. He said, "Can I leave early on Thursdays?"

Of course I had to ask why. Mike responded with, "I'm coaching a girls' soccer team."

Wow! an opportunity to market to our own youth sports customers that we had a coach in our own department. Of course, my answer to Mike's request was a resounding *yes*. He was even more motivated in his daily interactions with hundreds of customers. Even customer comments about Mike's support increased.

If others on the team thought Mike was receiving special treatment (which they did not), I would have responded by putting this question to them: "What do you want so that you, too, can advance your personal interests and growth as part of the job?"

*Personalize. Care. Positive results.* A winning combination.

# A Coffee Shop: What Happened When Nicholas Showed He Cared?

As I sat sipping my cup of coffee at the Lytton Roasting Company in Silicon Valley, a young lady ordered an assortment of coffees and pastries to take out.

As Nicholas, owner of the establishment, rang up the bill at the cash register, the lady sheepishly acknowledged that, "I forgot to bring my cash."

Nicholas did not hesitate. Although the patron was not a regular customer, Nicholas looked at her and said, "That's OK. You can pay me the next time you come in."

The astonished customer exclaimed, "Are you sure?"

Nicholas repeated what he had said earlier and the young lady's smile reflected that he had done the right thing.

I asked Nicholas about his philosophy and he said, "When you trust everyone you build partnerships with them. They understand that you *care* about them and will almost always come back."

What did I see the next day as I again sipped my coffee? The customer had returned—with two of her friends.

# Caring in this Hospital Setting

Linda, a very experienced nurse, described the situation in her hospital ward.

"There's a waiting list to work here in neo-natal intensive although the job can be very challenging," said Linda.

What was their secret in a setting which can often be frustrating to nurses?

Joan, the head nurse, had been there almost 20 years and always ensured there were fresh flowers, coffee and tea available.

If the unit was short-staffed, other nurses *volunteered* to help.

Joan let the nurses run the ward using their own best judgment about what worked for the patients.

At Christmas there were always at least 50 presents sent to her from the grateful staff.

There's more. The renal transplant physician called the nurses early each morning to tell them, "Thank you for taking care of my patients."

More common sense in action. It works.

# From Maverick to Caring Leader

Jim Waszak has had a number of senior management roles in manufacturing environments in the Midwest. He has a unique way of showing his employees that he *cares*. The positive results have manifested in increased productivity, teamwork and growth of employees.

Jim says, "A few years ago I was assigned the project of turning around a manufacturing operation. We had a guy named Roger who—as it turned out—was one of my problem children.

However at a company baseball game, I saw Roger show great leadership, enthusiasm and management skills.

I spoke with Roger about using the skills on the ball field in his day-to-day supervisory assignments. He allowed me to coach him and he turned into a real gem as a supervisor. He had previously been resistant to any feedback or coaching other than on the ball field.

The most touching moment occurred when I was leaving the organization. Roger gave me a big hug and said, 'I'm really going to miss you. You really changed my life.'"

His response was much more than I ever expected to hear.

*Caring, trust and empowerment.* Magical when used with love.

# I Want to be in Your Line at the Bank

I always ensured I was in Edward's line when I went into my local bank branch in Palo Alto. Edward was like Manda, who was commended earlier for her ability with e-mail personalization. He personalized our interaction, no matter how busy he was.

Edward had the knack of using his role as a teller to ensure my transaction was completed swiftly, and he also took the time to ask about my family—with his big smile. I always felt a little better than when the interaction began when I left Edward's area.

He said he had worked at a major retailer previously. They too always pushed their employees to be friendly to the customers. However, Edward quit.

Why?

"My boss acted arrogant and never took the time to even say 'hi' to me," said Edward.

Retention of employees. It can be costly for the most ridiculous reasons. Don't ever ask employees to do something and not hold management accountable to the same standards. Employees need to see that management *cares* via their actions.

# Listening in this Upscale Grocery = $$ and Loyalty

Sue has been employed in the upscale Piazza's Supermarket in Palo Alto for over 11 years and worked her way up to supervising the extensive cheese department.

Management decided to remodel the store, moving the cheese department away from its location in the center of the facility to a corner location. The new location would have less traffic and management felt it would still be a benefit to the store in the location.

Sue gave her input, preferring the old location, and ultimately accepted management's dictate regarding the change.

In the new location Sue discovered that the *regulars come to the new location; however, we are missing all the impulse buyers.*

Undaunted, Sue persisted with Gary Piazza, one of the three brothers who own the stores. She presented ideas that would be costly to once again remodel and move the cheese department to a more centralized location.

"I do know that Gary cares about our ideas," Sue stated, "and I was not willing to give up."

Management listened. The cheese department moved. Revenue increased.

Once again, a little *caring*, which allows ideas to be heard rather than squashed, paid off.

# Ouch! Fix this Quickly with a Little Caring

In his book *Primal Leadership*[34] Daniel Goleman confirms what I have found to be absolutely true:

**The number one reason people leave companies is dissatisfaction with the boss.**

# Two Suitcases, a Danish Accent and a Caring Customer Star

When I took on the role of Director of Customer Care for Privada, an Internet privacy company working with American Express, I quickly learned the value of Joel Peterson's advice to *be willing to be everyone's assistant no matter what role you have.*

---

34. Daniel Goleman, *Primal Leadership* (Harvard Business School Press, 1992)

We were fortunate to have a young lady named Malene in the organization. She had come from Denmark to the United States three years earlier, with only her two suitcases and no computer experience. Through perseverance, a quick wit and her technical acumen, Malene had risen to the lead technical support role.

Malene loved her work, saying, "There is nothing more wonderful than the joy of a customer who calls in upset about a technical problem—and I solve it for them. That makes my day." Malene was truly **caring in action**.

What can deter Malene? "When management does not listen to my personal needs or if management does not care whether or not I grow in my job." My role was to show Malene I cared about her growth—that's all she needed to be a customer star.

It worked too. Soon afterward the young lady from Denmark was featured nationally as the star of the month by the Help Desk Institute based on a testimonial I wrote. A full page appeared on their web site about Malene's positive attitude and her accomplishments.

When we had to play *David & Goliath* with the large and complex American Express support organization, it was Malene who again led the way. Our product was to be integrated into one of the Amex offerings and they would be the first to receive problem calls. They were also supporting many other vendors and products.

How could our little group of *Davids* gain priority treatment from this large international organization? When I went over the opportunity with Malene, she adamantly said, "Let me see those guys in person. I'll show them what we can do together. I'll show them that we really care about their success too."

That's all I needed to hear. Malene was off to Florida where she ensured that we could quickly establish a relationship with American Express service that would be mutually beneficial to our customers.

Complicated? Heck no—again, some trust and relationship-building that started with *I care*.

# Lands' End Keeps Its Word

In the days when Lands' End was an independent company I attended a national conference and listened to a talk by one of their marketing directors. The organization had a terrific reputation, and she expounded on their strong service philosophy—whereby they needed up to 1,000 representatives during peak holiday periods.

Being a bit skeptical about the marketing *hype*, I asked what criteria Lands' End used to measure the success of their representatives with customers—expecting the standard answer about how **quickly** they were able to take customer orders or solve issues.

The answer from marketing surprised me, "We measure our representatives on whether they spend *enough* time on the phones with customers. We want our customers to know that Lands' End is committed to the quality of its products and that we **care deeply** about our customer base."

That sounded good and I thought nothing more of it.

About two months later, my spouse was on the phone with a company and also speaking to our young daughter Kelly about the order. She set down the phone and began to measure Kelly to see if she was ordering the correct sizes.

I *had* to find out what was happening. I said "hello" and was greeted by Steve from Lands' End. When I asked him how he could take the time to wait on the phone. He said it was his responsibility to do whatever was necessary to satisfy the customer. He was not under the time pressure implemented by far too many companies to complete the call.

The order was completed successfully—and my daughter enjoyed her new clothes when they arrived.

Did Lands' End live by its word? Obviously, they did. *Caring internally and the trust it built led to caring externally—and customer loyalty and revenue.*

# 11 Conclusion

During the course of putting together *Care: You Have the Power* I have listened to perspectives regarding *care* from people in many areas of life. I have become even more intrigued with how much we are already demonstrating *care* in our society and how it could easily be expanded.

It would be a good idea to read the stories again to further comprehend the useful messages. The late Randy Pausch, professor at Carnegie Mellon University and author of *The Last Lecture* said, "Don't tell people how to live their lives. Just tell them stories. They will figure it out."[35]

A lady who serves meals at a facility geared to senior citizens told me she passed out about 100 meals a day and had been doing the job for 30 years. Her smile and enthusiasm has allowed patients to have a glimpse of *care* on over 700,000 occasions.

The warm greeting I received from a young bank teller I had not seen before certainly made me want to return. She said she interacts with customers about 20,000 times a year.

---

35. http://tinyurl.com/63dyp6

Both of the above scenarios reinforce the first impression that is created from a smile and the willingness to simply listen—and also the inherent motivation.

A young college student sitting next to me in a coffee shop stated that, *A caring teacher builds my self-esteem and makes me want to do better.* She was speaking about a professor who took at least a small amount of time to personalize his interactions with her.

The *care formula* is reflected within the stories in the book. *Trust is the glue in an organization*, per Warren Bennis and Burt Nanus *More trust equals more motivation and participation*, according to Bill Campbell.

What is the foundation that establishes trust? People feeling cared for and listened to. Keeping our word is another important component.

I noticed that the students of Allan Johnson, Director of Youth Programs at a training center in Menlo Park, California, were very attentive and responsive in his classes. Many of these students came from challenging situations.

"What are you doing differently?" I asked Allan.

He said, "I'm listening to the students. Many of them have not felt listened to for a long time."

Allan's previous experience included teaching high school for 18 years at inner-city high schools in Texas and Virginia. He took extra steps to build trust with the students. One school policy was that students had to have a pass to be in the hallway during class. Not in Allan's classes.

"If you need to go to the bathroom, just go," Allan told his students. "You don't need to raise your hand." He gave them this offer of respect on day one.

His youth did not spend extra time in the bathroom. In fact they changed dental appointments so they could attend class. Said Allan, "We had a 100% success rate and the students paid much more attention."

The opportunities are available in many professions, particularly in the medical field. When I visited my wonderful physician, Kathy Renschler, in Palo Alto, she always let me talk for a few minutes before asking about any physical ailments. Sometimes I felt so much better I almost forgot why I was there.

A few years ago I met a young mother and she said she took her two children to an excellent chiropractor who also coached them in nutrition. She said he always asked the children lots of questions and listened attentively to their answers. When I asked the doctor's name she said it was Bob Culver.

I was surprised. I had been going to Dr. Culver for years and he asked me few questions. On my next visit, I expressed my jealously and his response was, "You always tell me what is going on with your body. I don't need to ask many questions."

A great answer which also points out that listening is situational. Who are we listening to and what do they need? Personalize the interaction as we have witnessed in many stories in the book.

We always have a choice. If we are feeling down or perhaps in an organization where motivation is lacking, we have personal power to ensure those around us do feel care.

# About the Author

Ivan Temes is the founder of Leadership and Loyalty, a Palo Alto, California, based company dedicated to working with employees, leaders and personnel in transition to build confidence and customer and relationship skills.

Ivan's focus on *bringing out the star* within each person has produced outstanding results in arenas ranging from worldwide customer care at Levi's International, Apple Computer and other major companies, dotcoms and retail to a variety of non-profit, veterans and community organizations.

He has a BS Degree in Human Relations and Organizational Behavior from the University of San Francisco.

Ivan's unique perspective on care has also been gained from personal experiences associated with the downturns in life and a spiritual experience he had while in the emergency room at Stanford Hospital in 2001.

Ivan would like to hear from you and invites you to share your stories on the power of caring. Please send any Care stories you would like to share with him to: care@ivantemes.com.

# Create Thought Leadership for your Company

Books deliver instant credibility to the author. Having an MBA or Ph.D. is great; however, putting the word "author" in front of your name is similar to using the letters Ph.D. or MBA. You are no long Michael Green, you are "Author Michael Green."

Books give you a platform to stand on. They help you to:

- Demonstrate your thought leadership
- Generate leads

Books deliver increased revenue, particularly indirect revenue:

- A typical consultant will make 3x in indirect revenue for every dollar they make on book sales

Books are better than a business card. They are:

- More powerful than white papers
- An item that makes it to the book shelf vs. the circular file
- The best tschocke you can give at a conference

# Why Wait to Write Your Book?

Check out other companies that have built credibility by writing and publishing a book through Happy About.

Contact Happy About at 408-257-3000 or go to http://happyabout.info.

# Other Happy About® Books

Purchase these books at Happy About
http://happyabout.info
or at other online and physical bookstores.

*Bring Humor and Laughter Back into Life!*

If you can develop your sense of humor and learn to laugh at yourself daily, I guarantee you will feel like the most successful person on Earth.

Paperback $16.95
eBook $11.95

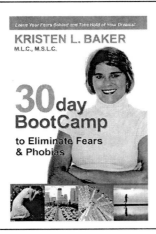

*30day BootCamp to Eliminate Fears & Phobias*

This book is an interactive book that will help you to overcome your fears and phobias, by defining, changing your thought process, gaining self-confidence and believing in yourself.

Paperback $19.95
eBook $11.95

### *Happy About Customer Service?*

This book will develop your customer service standards so that you consistently, and to the endless pleasure of your customers, will deliver Customer Service Excellence.

Paperback $19.95
eBook $11.95

### *42 Rules™ for Working Moms*

This book assembles the guidance of contributors who offer their thoughts on topics ranging from raising polite children and making time for yourself, as well as your mate, to losing the mommy guilt and delegating at home.

Paperback $19.95
eBook $11.95

## Additional Praise for this Book

"I think this book is a wonderful testimony to Ivan's devotion to care."
**James Thomas, Reverend and Psychologist**

"It was so great to read this book—I wish it was mandatory reading for all upper management folks."
**Manda Choi, Customer Care Representative**

"While watching my Dad put together his book, I not only saw the pages come to life, I saw Dad come to life. Dad had a new perspective on life, a way to teach people about caring. *Care: You Have the Power* isn't all about Dad, nor is it all about care—it's also about how people interact with care—how they use it, how they waste it and how they fix it.

Many of the stories in this book have come from negative experiences that could have been avoided with a sprinkle of care. When I attended one of Dad's seminars I saw how much he wanted to share the notion of care. Dad really seemed to connect with these people in transition.

Dad gets the care principle—that care is a combination of many different things. As this book progressed, so did Dad. He poured his heart and soul into completing this book and I'm positive you will reap the rewards of caring in every part of your lives."
**Josh Temes (age 13)**